OPPORTUNITIES IN
LAW CAREERS

Gary A. Munneke

 **VGM Career Horizons**
A Division of National Textbook Company
8259 Niles Center Road, Skokie, Illinois 60077

Cover photo: Wide World Photos.

ABOUT THE AUTHOR

Gary A. Munneke is presently Assistant Dean and Assistant Professor of the Delaware Law School of Widener University, Wilmington, Delaware. From 1973-1980, he served as Assistant Dean and Director of Placement at the University of Texas School of Law in Austin, Texas. A native of Cedar Rapids, Iowa, Dean Munneke graduated from high school in Houston, Texas. He attended the University of Texas at Austin, graduating in 1970 with a B.A. in Psychology, and in 1973 with a J.D. from the University of Texas School of Law.

Dean Munneke has been an active member of the State Bar of Texas since 1973. He has served on numerous committees in the American Bar Association, including the Standing Committee on Professional Utilization and Career Development and the Task Force on the National Conference on the Role of the Lawyer in the 1980s. He has also chaired the ABA Young Lawyers Division Committee on Career Planning and Placement and the General Practice Section Committee on New Lawyers. He served as President of the National Association for Law Placement in 1977-78, and has written and lectured extensively in the field of legal career development.

ACKNOWLEDGEMENTS

I wish to thank Adrienne Diehr, the Editorial Director for the Placement Office at the University of Texas Law School, whose sage advice seems always to lead me to a more readable product. Her suggestions during this project have been invaluable. I wish to thank the ABA Standing Committee on Professional Utilization and Career Development, and especially staff liaison, Frances Utley. They led me into this undertaking, and were always ready to give advice when asked. I wish to thank the many professional colleagues in the law placement field, in legal education, and in the legal profession, because only constant contact with these others can provide an author the depth of experience to create a work like this. I wish to thank the hundreds of pre-law students, law students, and practicing lawyers who have come to me for advice about their careers, because they have provided constant reminders of what opportunities there are in the world for lawyers as well as the pitfalls that await the unaware.

I also wish to acknowledge the work of Dana Jones Massey, who was responsible for the typing of the manuscript.

Author's Note

This book has been reviewed by the Standing Committee on Professional Utilization and Career Development of the American Bar Association. The Standing Committee recommends that all pre-law students give careful consideration to the possibilities in a legal career as presented in this book and undertake serious career planning before making the commitment to go to law school. Since 1972, the Standing Committee has maintained: "There is no conclusive evidence to indicate that there are now, or are likely to be in the foreseeable future, more legally trained men and women than can be satisfactorily and productively employed. The existence of a large pool of well-qualified, legally trained individuals constitutes a major opportunity and should be viewed as a significant national resource." However, this does not mean that the job market for new lawyers will not be limited in some areas that are more popular either professionally or geographically.

CONTENTS

   The large law firm. The medium law firm. The small
   law firm. Legal clinics: group and prepaid services.
   The sole practitioner.

   The corporate law department. Law-related corporate
   positions. Non-legal corporate positions.

   Federal regulatory agency lawyers. State agency
   lawyers. Local government lawyers. Military lawyers.
   Lawyers in the legislative branch. Judges and clerks.
   Public administrators.

   Indigent legal services lawyers. Lawyers with public
   interest groups. Private practitioners and *pro-bono*
   work.

   Teaching in law school. Teaching outside law school.
   Law libraries. Lawyers in educational administration.
   Lawyers in research and publishing.

Overleaf: Entrance to the law library, University of Texas at Austin.
Photo: Frank Armstrong.

CHAPTER 1

INTRODUCTION

At a party not long ago, I saw a number of old friends. We had all gone our separate ways since school, and this reunion was a chance to share experiences and catch up on old times. We made an interesting group; a casual observer might wonder what brought us all together. Although we were all lawyers, our careers and our lives had taken many different and sometimes unconventional paths.

In one corner, two women and two men were involved in an animated discussion. The most vocal member of the group was Diana, a former high school and college debater who had decided to go to law school. Diana was an activist; her fingers were in every pie. She was articulate, and a formidable opponent for all who dared to take her on. After law school, Diana had taken a job with one of the largest and most prestigious firms in the country as a trial lawyer. She has worked tirelessly to develop and perfect those natural skills of speaking and persuasion that she first demonstrated back in school.

Carol stood across from Diana and followed the conversation thoughtfully, occasionally interjecting a pertinent comment. In law school, Carol had been the intellectual of our group. Married to a college professor, and a product of academia, she was totally at ease in the intellectual jousting tournament of law school. Carol's greatest asset was her profound grasp of deductive reasoning, which enabled her to fathom even the most complex issue. After graduation, Carol gravitated toward a career with a public

1

interest law firm, where she now researches and analyzes trend-setting litigation.

Like Carol, Dave stood and listened thoughtfully, almost as if he were taking notes, and only occasionally volunteered agreement or objection. Dave was an analyst too, but unlike Carol and Diana, he never practiced law and never intended to. He was a reporter both before he came to law school and after. With his background in law and journalism, he became a correspondent covering, among other things, legal issues for a national news magazine. Earlier in the evening everyone had been congratulating him on his new position as managing editor of a national legal newspaper.

The person most actively engaged in the discussion with Diana was Ted, who could best be called an entrepreneur. A century earlier, Ted might have made his fortune peddling snake oil or magic elixir. During law school and for the first couple of years thereafter, he created a consumer research organization and persuaded literally thousands of people to join his cause. Then he went into the magazine business. Unlike Dave, Ted knew nothing about journalism or publishing, but his friend Mike did. Mike, also a lawyer, had started a magazine when he got out of law school. It became one of the most successful magazines in publishing history. Ted joined the staff as associate publisher, and is now manager of circulation and special editions.

In another corner stood Elliott, Bill, and Sheila, all of whom had been notably ambitious and energetic as students. Elliott, the social organizer of the class, had taken a traditional route, going into practice with a fairly large patent law firm. A former engineer, he had rejected that career because he felt that engineers were "too stuffy." Elliott now works for the patent section of a corporate law department.

After law school Bill went into private practice with a small firm. In his firm, the lawyers didn't specialize, but handled whatever walked through the door. No two days were the same, and the pressure was tremendous. Bill always took the burden of each client's problem upon himself, and there were numerous clients. After five years, Bill craved regular hours and a peaceful routine; and he left the law firm for a nine-to-five government job doing legal research for a judge.

Then there was Sheila, a cool northeasterner who didn't find out until after law school that she actually loved the conflict of the courtroom. She became a prosecutor in a city attorney's office. Many other people are like Bill; they dislike the tension associated with representing clients in an adversary system. Sheila found that she thrived on it.

In the center of the room, Charles, Sam, David, John, and Alice were loudly debating the merits of a recent Supreme Court decision involving the rights of minorities and women. Charles, the discussion leader, had gone to work for the federal government as soon as he graduated from law school. His work with a large regulatory agency provided an outlet for his often-expressed desire to help society. Another factor in his decision to go to Washington was "Potomac fever," and a longing to see more of the world than his home community.

Sam, on the other hand, had elected to enter practice in a predominantly black neighborhood. Sam had become a college debater in the South at a time when educational opportunities for blacks were less than spectacular. The year after graduation, he accepted a fellowship with a national civil rights organization. His practice today, while quite broad, still maintains its civil rights flavor.

While still in law school, David had become a legislative aide in the state legislature. He had held a series of jobs, each with greater influences than the last. David's success was also attributable to a series of shrewd political guesses as to where the power was likely to shift. We all expected him to be running for office himself sometime soon.

One of the most enigmatic figures in our class was John, a West Point graduate who became an outspoken critic of the Vietnam war. As a public interest lawyer, he was so persuasive that he was hired by a major university as its lobbyist. Just when everyone thought that John had "arrived" at the pinnacle of his career, he quit his job to go back to school for his L.L.M., a graduate law degree. He was just stopping by the reunion briefly before flying to Washington, D.C., where he would be working for a prestigious international agency.

Alice was a public defender. A good friend of Carol in law school, Alice had always lived in her friend's intellectual shadow. After graduation, Alice took a job in a western state where she began to establish her own identity. Within four years, she had become the director of the entire public defender's office, where she supervised a staff of more than twenty other lawyers.

Gary, Ed, and Tim stood near the punch bowl laughing and reminiscing. Although close friends in school, they had not seen much of each other since graduation. Gary went to work for the state bar association in the general counsel's office. He investigates grievances against other lawyers including, unfortunately, a couple of former classmates who perhaps failed to study their ethics well enough in law school.

Ed, whom we called "the General," was actually a Major in the U. S. Army Judge Advocate General Corps. Many lawyers serve in the JAGC to fulfill the ROTC commitment and then get out. Ed, to the contrary, enjoyed his military life and intended to make a career of it.

The party would not have seemed complete without Tim, the rugged individualist. Unlike the other practicing attorneys at the party, no one paid Tim's salary. After working for a government agency and a corporation, he decided to be his own boss and follow the time-honored professional tradition of "hanging out his shingle." It has been tough going thus far for Tim, but he is beginning to see the fruits of his labor, and he really appreciates his independence.

Like any group at a class reunion, we all laughed, relived old times, and asked about absent friends. Our classmates had gone into every conceivable type of law practice, insurance companies, accounting firms, and banks. There were educators (teachers, administrators, librarians, researchers) in law schools and universities. There were idle philanthrophists and active philanderers. There were also two suicides no one could explain.

The one fact apparent to everyone at the party was that the work of legally trained people is as broad as the endeavors of human beings. Whatever people do in this complex world, there will be legal problems and lawyers to help solve them. Lawyers come in all shapes, races, and personalities. They work in a multitude of environments.

All the people described at the party are real and were class-mates of the author. As a group, they have come a long way since the early seventies when they were law students. They have shed their blue jeans, and have developed in the succeeding years an amazing sophistication. They have come far, and yet they still have their finest years ahead of them. The average lawyer has a professional life of forty years, so this group has thirty to thirty-five years to go.

Judging by the experiences of this group, the prospective law student might do well to consider *careers in law* rather than *a career as a lawyer*. This book examines many of those careers. It discusses what lawyers in these various careers do, how they attain their positions, and the opportunities available for future lawyers.

In addition to discussing legal careers, this book covers other topics such as: admission to law school, elements of legal education, finding a job after graduation, financial and other rewards, and fields to consider if law school is not possible.

A legal education is rigorous and lengthy, and requires tre-mendous commitment. It is not something to be "tried" as a possibility by those who are attempting to find out what to do with their lives. The reader is encouraged to use the information in this book to help make the best possible career decision.

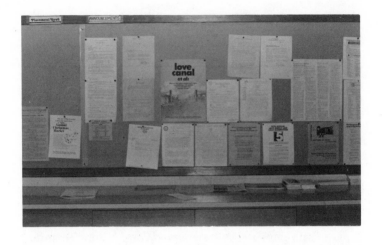

The placement office and library provide information about multitudes of choices in law careers. Photo: Delaware Law School, Widener University, Wilmington, Delaware.

CHAPTER 2

OPPORTUNITIES IN LAW:
AN OVERVIEW

A legal education prepares one for an almost unlimited array of career opportunities. Knowledge of the law is useful in most aspects of life and necessary in some. In a complex society, contact with the law becomes increasingly harder to avoid. Businesses and individuals alike are required to turn to lawyers simply to exist.

When you have been trained in the law, the use to which your law degree can be put is limited only by your own imagination and your awareness of the opportunities. Unfortunately, many persons who are considering law are woefully unprepared to make the decision to get a legal education because they do not really know what lawyers do. They are unaware of the vast employment possibilities open to them and they lack the self-knowledge to enable them to make a rational career decision. Career choices should be suited to a person's individual abilities, goals, and values. For some, the most desirable choice might be to practice with a large law firm in a large city—for others this might be the worst possible alternative. It is entirely a matter of personal choice. This book attempts to insure that the decision will be a carefully thought-out one, and not one hastily made as a result of ignorance of alternatives.

The following chapters illustrate some of the typical career alternatives available to lawyers today. The list is by no means

7

exclusive. Before proceeding to discuss specific opportunities, it may be useful to the reader to take a broad look at the legal profession.

The amount of formal research on lawyers and the profession is relatively small. When we try to compile statistical information, it is much like putting together a giant jigsaw puzzle with a lot of missing pieces. There are, however, some things that are known about the legal profession.

Sometime in 1979, for the first time in history, there were more than 500,000 men and women licensed to practice law—one half million people. No nation in history has had as many lawyers to solve its problems.

In fact, no one knows exactly how many lawyers there are so 500,000 is an educated guess. In 1951, there were 221,605 lawyers according to the ABA 1971 *Lawyer Statistical Report.* By 1970, the number had increased to 335,242. From 1970 to 1979, roughly 327,000 new lawyers were licensed. The American Bar Association reported that there were 480,886 in December 1979, taking reports from the various states which in some instances did not include the most recent licensees.

The U. S. Census Bureau estimated the U. S. population to be approximately 222,000,000 in 1979. This means that there is in our country one lawyer for every 440 people. Since the ratio was 1/696 in 1950 and 1/572 in 1970, it is apparent that the rate of growth in the profession has been much greater than in the general population. Part of this may be attributed to the fact that lawyers do not just work for people; they work for business, private associations, and the government. All these entities use legal services, and so, while a ratio of 1/1000 is not unusual in a rural area where most of the legal work is done for individuals, the ratio drops dramatically in urban areas, where a ratio of 1/230 would not be unusual. Thus, when viewed in the light of the urbanization of society, in terms of both complexity and demographic movement of the population to the cities, the drop in the lawyer/population ratio is not surprising. However, the United States still has more lawyers per capita than any other nation including the industrialized countries.

In 1951, 86.8 percent of the lawyers were in private practice. The figure had dropped to 76.2 percent by 1960 and 72.7 percent by 1970. During the same period, the percentage of attorneys in government service increased from 13.4 percent in both 1950 and 1960 to 14.3 percent in 1970, and in private organizations such as corporations from 6.3 percent in 1950 to 9.9 percent in 1960 to 12.4 percent in 1970. (The totals do not total 100 percent due to some overlap in categories.)

Since 1976, the National Association for Law Placement (NALP) has surveyed the graduates of the nation's law schools to get an annual employment report. While NALP uses more categories than private practice, government service, and private organizations, it is possible to describe the NALP data in that way. Thus, for each year since 1976, the percentage of lawyers entering private practice has been around 60 percent. The percentage entering government positions has been about 22 percent, and the percentage entering private organizations about 18 percent.

The NALP employment figures suggest that the percentage of lawyers in private practice has continued to drop during the 1970s, and that, given the large number of new lawyers graduating during the decade, the percentage of all lawyers may look something like this in 1980: private practice 67 percent, government 18 percent, and private organizations 15 percent.

It is undeniable, however, that the face of the profession has changed so rapidly that it would be of little value to draw inferences about the nature of law practice from data collected in 1960 or 1970.

There have been other changes, too. Among those in private practice, 67.9 percent were sole practitioners in 1951. By 1960, the percentage had dropped to 60.8 percent and to 50.3 percent in 1970. The number of recent law graduates "hanging out their own shingle" has dropped to a paltry 5 percent according to NALP. Even if we assume that many lawyers do embark upon individual practices after several years with a law firm, it is likely that fewer than 30 percent of the nation's lawyers practice by themselves today. On the other hand, not only have more lawyers been practicing in firms, but the firms themselves have been getting bigger. In 1973, there were only a few firms in the U. S. with more than 50 lawyers. They accounted for less than 1 percent of the private bar. In 1979, such large firms represented 4-5 percent of the private practitioners in the U. S. and there are over 200 firms with 50 lawyers or more.

While the organization of the law office has changed dramatically, that change pales when compared to the increased numbers of women who have entered the legal profession. In 1951, there were 5,493 women lawyers (2.5 percent); by 1970, there were 9,956 (almost 3 percent). In the late sixties, more women became interested in legal careers. In 1970, there were 7,031 women enrolled in law school. By 1976, the figure had reached 36,808, or 30 percent of all students in law school. By looking at the number of women who have graduated from law school since 1970, we can estimate that there are some 65,000 women lawyers today, or 13 percent of all lawyers. The figure should reach 25 percent by 1990. The enrollment of minority students has increased from 2,933 in 1970 to 9,922 in 1978. This is a substantial increase, but not as dramatic as the increase in the number of women law students.

The size of the profession is undoubtedly going to grow for many years to come. The National Conference of Bar Examiners reports 41,662 admissions to the bar in 1978, up over 4,000 from the year before. Law school enrollment will probably not decline for a number of years. An average lawyer's career will span 40 years, and the number of retirement-age lawyers is significantly smaller than the number of new admittees. Therefore, we can expect the profession to continue to grow statistically younger as well as larger in the next decade. (In 1979, roughly one-half the lawyers were 36 years of age or younger.)

It is also true that there will be fewer young adults in college between now and the turn of the century. This may mean that it will be somewhat easier to gain admission to law school than in the past decade, although the number of law students will probably not drop, since there are now so many more applicants than there are law school seats. If anything, competition among schools for the best students will increase.

Overleaf: The private practitioner spends much time alone, drafting documents for clients. Photo: G. Munneke.

CHAPTER 3

THE PRIVATE PRACTITIONER

The most vocal member of the group was Diana, a former high school and college debater who had decided to go to law school. Diana was an activist; her fingers were in every pie. She was articulate, and a formidable opponent for all who dared to take her on. After law school, Diana had taken a job with one of the largest and most prestigious law firms in the country as a trial lawyer. She has worked tirelessly to develop and perfect those natural skills of speaking and persuasion she first demonstrated back in school.

What is a private practitioner? Most people have images of lawyers that have been established by the mass media as well as by personal experience. To most of us, the term "private practitioner" is in many ways synonymous with the word "lawyer." Today, although many lawyers do not engage in private practice, it is still a fact that the majority of lawyers are private practitioners.

Before proceeding, it might be helpful to define private practice. As used here, the term means an individual or organization engaged in the business of delivering legal services. Lawyers who practice alone are often called "sole practitioners." Groups of lawyers are called firms. The firm is usually a partnership and members of the firm are the partners. Some firms may be organized as professional corporations and the members called shareholders. In either case, the members of the firm are the experienced attorneys. In most firms, there are younger or more inexperienced salaried attorneys called "associates."

It is also important to note that lawyers are in the *business* of delivering legal services. Practicing law is a business, and like any business, the practicing lawyer has a product to sell. That product is legal services. Lawyers have overhead expenses—space, equipment, staff, library, and other expenses that may gobble up 50 percent of the gross receipts each month. Thus, the lawyer's income depends on how much work he or she puts in, how much he or she is willing to charge for his or her time, and how efficiently the law office is managed.

A lawyer is not just a businessperson, however, but is also a professional whose responsibilities go beyond merely making a profit. An attorney is an officer of the courts in the state where that person is licensed, and as such is charged with a duty to uphold the laws and to act in such a way as to see that justice is done. In the 1970s, the legal profession was challenged from both within and without by those who felt that too many lawyers were ignoring their professional responsibilities to clients and the public. The Watergate era demonstrated to the American people that some lawyers were willing and able to use and abuse the legal system to achieve their own ends.

It would be naive to suggest that Watergate was somehow responsible for a downturn in the public's opinion of lawyers. In truth, Watergate merely confirmed the worst suspicions of many. The "shyster" lawyer is a part of our American folklore. Who among us could not relate some story of a bad experience that we or someone we know has had with a lawyer?

Even before this country was founded, lawyers were perceived as dishonest. In Shakespeare's play *Henry VI Part 2* one of the rebels against the king urges that when the revolution comes, "the first thing we do, let's kill all the lawyers." Many writers have dreamed of utopias where lawyers would not be needed to settle disputes.

Fortunately or not, depending upon your point of view, life is not without disputes. Conflict is a seemingly inevitable outgrowth of human interaction. And as long as there is human conflict, there will be lawyers. Undoubtedly there will always be some lawyers who abuse the system and some people who will always believe that lawyers are crooks. In reality, most lawyers are dedicated and conscientious advocates of justice. Our legal system, for all its flaws, is better than the alternative. Imagine for a minute a society without laws. If someone wronged you, you would just have to take care of it yourself. If some squatters moved onto your land, you would have to evict them by force. If someone ran into your car causing you bodily injury, you would have to extract compensation by force if necessary. If a husband and wife split up, they would have to fight out the property settlement. If there were no criminal laws, you would have to punish those who wronged you, a situation that would present no problems if you happened to be six feet eight, two hundred fifty pounds and mean as a prairie rattlesnake. Most of us aren't six feet eight, however.

In a society governed by the rule of law, "dedicated to the purpose that men are endowed by their creator with certain unalienable rights," and committed to a system which provides for the adjudication of those rights in an orderly way, lawyers are not only useful, but necessary. The legal services that lawyers sell may be the only way the average citizen can assert or vindicate his rights. The broad general heading of *private practice* encompasses many possibilities, from the sole practitioner in a small town, to the position of associate with a firm of more than one-hundred in a large city, and given this diversity, the advantages and disadvantages of each situation must be looked at individually with the realization that no solution will be a problem-free one.

Small firm practice is the backbone of the system of legal representation in the United States. Unlike many other areas in the business community, law firms have not grown to the point of employing thousands of individuals. The largest law firm in the world in 1979 was Baker and McKenzie, with a main office in Chicago and branches throughout the world. Fourteen law firms were large enough to employ more than 200 lawyers, and 200 firms had 50 or more. Together, all of these large law firms account for no more than 5 percent of the practicing bar. While the number of lawyers in these large organizations appears to be increasing, the number of sole practitioners declined from two-thirds of all lawyers in private practice in 1950 to under one-half in 1970, according to the *Lawyer Statistical Report* produced by the American Bar Foundation.

Most firms have fewer than five attorneys, and in all but the largest cities in the United States, a law firm with more than ten attorneys is considered large. For our purposes, small firms are those with less than ten attorneys. Most law firms hire at least as many non-legal personnel as they do lawyers, and some hire more than that.

What is it about the small firm that makes it attractive? Probably the biggest factor is personal freedom. Unfettered by bureaucratic rules or the sometimes impersonal environments of some large organizations, lawyers in small firms often feel freer to set their own hours, make meaningful choices about their careers, and establish personal relationships with clients sooner in their professional development. In a large firm, client contact may be postponed for several years after graduation from law school; the lawyer in the small firm may have client contact the first day.

Another factor is that the prospects for partnership are better and the time frame before consideration shorter in small firms. Large firms usually do not consider associates for partnership until six or more years' association with the firm. Although the decision to join a small firm will probably mean a lower starting salary and possibly less money over the long haul, many are willing to accept less money because of other benefits. For instance, the attrition rate is greater in large firms which often hire two to three times the number of associates than will ever make partner. This can cause intense competition and considerable insecurity among those hired. The insecurity of a small firm practice often comes from inadequate training and supervision, as well as a scarcity of regular clients.

Some of those who choose a small firm practice are interested in doing this in an urban setting, and face the problem of competing with the abundance of talent and resources available to their larger counterparts. The small firm also has lure for those who are tired of the problems and inconveniences of urban life, and are interested in living in rural areas, in which case the large firms are non-existent.

Whether or not the small firm in a small town is an attractive option would depend in large part on the attitude of the individual. Some might consider the small town setting to be a positive consideration, others would eliminate this type of practice simply because they prefer to live in a city, either for the variety of activity it offers, or for the increased possibility for professional recognition.

There are quite a few other factors to be considered, not the least of which would be the type of practice being done. Many small firms are not able to specialize because the available clients necessitate a more general practice, or because the expense of maintaining resources for specialized research and consultation might prove at times to be too much of a burden. However, some small firms do have very specialized practices, particularly in the large cities.

Yet another factor that makes small firms' practice alluring is the familiar nature of the professional relationships. Where attorneys work together closely on a daily basis, they frequently develop close personal relationships. Older attorneys are more likely to develop something akin to a parental relationship with young lawyers in the small firm. While such close relationships tend to produce firms where the lawyers are not diverse politically, socially, or otherwise, it is comforting to many new lawyers to have such role models. One result of the closer relationship is that associates often have greater input into major decisions of the firm than they would in a large firm.

The smallest of the small firms is the individual or sole practitioner. The sole practitioner is to many people the prototype of their image of what a lawyer is like. The Perry Mason character created by Erle Stanley Gardner (himself a lawyer) and further popularized on television is an obvious example. With no more than his trusty secretary, Della Street, faithful investigator, Paul Drake, and a just cause, Perry sallies out to do battle with his arch-enemy, Hamilton Burger, the hapless District Attorney. The image, although over-glamorized, has some basis in fact. Many have chosen to go it alone because they are fiercely independent and responsible to no one but their clients, who are for the most part individuals. As a rule, businesses hire law firms (and the bigger the business, the bigger the firm hired), while individuals hire individual lawyers. Despite their declining numbers, the sole practitioner will probably never disappear from the legal scene.

Today, however, it is difficult to be a self-employed lawyer. Only 5% of recent law graduates elect to go into individual private practice directly after law school according to the National Association for Law Placement (NALP).

There are financial reasons for the small number of sole practitioners. The high cost of doing business today inflates overhead and the economy of scale which is possible in larger organizations gives larger firms a competitive edge. Sole practitioners may discover that client demands may leave them with less freedom of choice about their lifestyles than they would hope. Anyone with a legal problem who walks in the door is a client but there is always the possibility that one day no clients will come in the door. Many sole practitioners at some time choose to engage in practice with one or more other attorneys if only to share expenses.

Because the percentage of sole practitioners has decreased— from 24 percent to 19 percent of the private bar in Chicago between 1950 and 1970 according to one survey, some observers of the legal profession have pronounced the sole practitioner dead. He may be ill, but he is certainly not dead. The number of sole practitioners has actually increased, and with some demographers predicting an increase in small town and rural population for the first time since the turn of the century, there may well be a growth of this fiercely independent breed in the coming decades.

Once a law firm reaches a size of around ten lawyers, it begins to undergo a metamorphosis. What had been a loosely knit organization begins to become institutionalized. Partners and associates who formerly would work for clients and develop areas of expertise in a more or less informal way begin to find themselves imposing more structure on the firm, assigning new lawyers to certain areas, and often forming sections or departments. While organization and management of the firm were handled once without much planning or coordination by the lawyers, they now find that they must hire specialists (e.g., an office manager, librarian, recruiting administrator) to give themselves more time to practice law. While hiring was always done in a haphazard and unplanned way, it becomes more regular and time-consuming as the firm grows larger.

The medium-sized or transitional firm is probably the most interesting firm from an organizational point of view. It is always changing, and while both very large and very small firms tend to be fairly predictable in their organizational patterns, medium-sized firms are not. They may try to stay as informal as possible as long as they can, or they may develop formal organizational patterns at a relatively small size. They may grow into large firms, remain stable for years, or completely splinter into several small firms.

Like the large firms, transitional firms are primarily creatures of the big city. Very few firms of more than ten lawyers can be found outside big cities. However, in mid-sized cities of roughly 100,000 to 1,000,000, the largest firms may be what are described here as medium-sized firms.

The largest firms are those with over 50 lawyers. These firms are located in the major cities. They frequently have long-standing prestigious reputations, and clients to match. In fact, firms generally grow to such a size to accommodate the needs of large corporate clients: banks, insurance companies, industrials, as well as large private estates and organizations.

A large firm tends to have a tight hierarchical structure. There is a partnership which may include any number of the lawyers in the firm, from almost half to only one-fourth. The partnership is most often governed by a management committee, although in many patriarchal firms a managing partner retains many powers and prerogatives. In many firms, the law firm administrator who oversees a staff of hundreds assumes many of the responsibilities of the managing partner. Most firms have a committee system to spread out policy decisions and work. These committees may or may not include associates.

The associates are the salaried lawyers in the firm. Although there is some inevitable attrition, many of the associates (and this varies from firm to firm) can expect to be considered for partnership after six to eight years.

Larger firms tend to provide greater opportunities for specialization, the highest initial starting salaries, and a sense of security and a chance to practice law with other attorneys who are generally able to provide the benefit of valuable experience. The problems of being an associate with a big firm cannot be overlooked either. In recent years these problems have been a source of increasing concern to law school graduates who want freedom in both the hours they work and the kinds of clients they handle. The advantages and disadvantages of small firm/small town vs. large firm/large city could be discussed almost endlessly. There are, of course, the choices that represent some compromise between these two ends of the spectrum in the medium-sized firms in both small and large cities, which incorporate some of the good and bad features of both.

The choice is not an easy one, and is certainly a highly personal one that can be made only by you. All we can hope to do is to provoke thought on the question, and perhaps raise questions on each that must be answered before any decision is made. Whatever the choice, it will have a profound effect on both your personal and professional life. The decision is not one that should be made hastily or on the basis of hearsay, but rather should be made logically, based on careful consideration of facts. It is possible that you would find the entire prospect of private practice undesirable and would find much greater satisfaction in one of the other areas of legal or non-legal practice.

Overleaf: Leonard Williamson, chairperson of the National Bar Association Patent Law Section and a patent attorney with The Proctor & Gamble Co., discusses problems of patent licensing abroad in a symposium on "International Trade Agreements." Photo: Julia Jones.

CHAPTER 4

CORPORATE LAW

> Elliott had taken a traditional route, going into prac-
> tice with a fairly large patent law firm. A former
> engineer, he had rejected that career because he felt
> that engineers were "too stuffy." Elliott now works
> for the patent section of a corporate law department.

Practicing law in and for a corporation as a career is a choice
made by approximately 10% of the new graduates of approved
law schools each year. This corresponds to approximately 10.3%
of the organized bar who are actually engaged in corporate
practice. In this decade, however, the changes in corporate
practice may overshadow all other changes in the legal profession.

Despite the number of corporation lawyers, many people
could not explain what it is one does. Because they tend to maintain a rather low profile, corporation lawyers are often not
considered by people when they think about what lawyers do.
Another reason for this ignorance may be that lawyers' roles
in corporations are so varied that it is more difficult to formulate
a picture of a "typical" corporation lawyer than it would be for
a lawyer in some other area.

The number of attorneys employed by the corporation will
vary widely with the size and type of the corporation. Many
smaller and some large corporations farm out all their legal
problems to private firms. Many others have in-house counsel

for only certain matters. Other corporations have a legal staff large enough to handle most legal problems in-house.

In a small corporation, an attorney may have responsibility other than the legal affairs of the business. An increasing number of corporations are seeking young lawyers to handle legal problems and assume management duties, too. Whether there is a legal staff, or an individual full-time lawyer employed by the corporation, the chief legal officer in a corporation is usually referred to as the general counsel.

Some corporations also hire lawyers outside their regular legal departments. Oil companies typically have lawyers in exploration or land departments totally distinct from their legal departments. Some companies hire attorneys in tax departments, in research and development, and in other capacities which require an ability to deal with the law.

The corporate legal department, whether it is one lawyer or 973 as in the case of American Telephone and Telegraph Company, can best be understood as a "kept" law firm. A private law firm usually has many clients, but a corporate law department has only one—that corporation. For whom, then, does the lawyer in a corporation work? The answer depends in part upon where in the corporation's organizational chart the legal department is located. However, it is not uncommon for the general counsel or chief legal officer to report to the president or chief executive officer. Most corporate law departments have, in addition to a general counsel, associate general counsels corresponding to partners in a law firm in terms of experience, and assistant general counsels corresponding to associates. Lawyers in the legal department may work with executives in different sectors of management, on a regular basis or only sporadically. As in the case of large law firms, corporate law departments of more than a few lawyers tend to be departmentalized.

There are some interesting ethical questions that may arise in corporate practice. How far does the lawyer's privilege of confidentiality in communication with a client extend if the client is so nebulously defined? In cases involving white collar crime, can a lawyer represent both the corporation and an individual employee in a criminal case without compromising one or the other?

Briefly comparing life in a corporation to life in a law firm, the corporate lawyer comes out favorably. In terms of salary, the median salary is probably somewhat higher than in firms. The top salaries are no higher than the top salaries for law firms, but the bottom salaries are not as low. Fringe benefits also tend to be better in the corporation. Because even the smallest business corporation often employs more people than the largest law firm, the insurance, retirement, and other fringes will often be more generous in the corporation. Corporations may offer stock options or other financial opportunities a firm would not.

Other advantages to a corporate job include hours, options, and mobility. In a law firm the lawyer is the unit of production. Your income is based on the number of hours you work for clients times your hourly rate of billing, less overhead costs. In a company, there is some other product which earns the money; the lawyers are an expense. Thus if the corporation needs 120 hours of legal work it is as easy to hire three lawyers at 40 hours per week as two lawyers at 60 hours per week. While a lawyer's first few years in a firm may necessitate working 60 hours or more weekly, the corporate lawyer usually follows typical nine-to-five hours. In the case of career options, there are many more places to move in a corporate entity both laterally and vertically, than in a law firm. Many top managers, including a significant number of chief executive officers of major corporations, are lawyers. An individual who wants to move into management in a corporation, particularly a larger one, can usually do so. The last factor mentioned here is mobility. For the lawyer willing to move around the country, working in a corporate law department may provide opportunities for seeing new places.

This is a benefit that only a few law firms can offer. Of course, the opportunity to travel will be dependent upon the size and dispersion of the corporation's law department. For instance, a large company may have operations in many locations throughout the United States and abroad. It is increasingly common to have lawyers at each plant or branch location who can handle the myriad questions that arise daily in the course of business.

Contrasting the large and small corporate law department, there are some significant differences. As in the case of law firms, salaries tend to be better in larger organizations. More important, however, are differences in responsibilities. The large law department may be thought of as a large law firm that is owned by the corporation. Instead of working for a number of different clients, the corporate attorney works for only one. However, in a large corporation, the company operations may be so diverse that the attorney has the feeling that he or she works for a number of clients. In any event, the lawyer in the large corporation is probably a specialist. In fact, the attorney in a large corporate law department often has a practice that is much closer to that of an attorney in a large law firm than the lawyer in a small firm. By the same token, the practice in a small corporate law department may be more like that in a small firm than in a larger corporation.

The small corporate law department may offer some unusual opportunities for a law graduate. The lawyer is likely to be more closely involved in the running of the business, in such things as determining policy and becoming involved in management. In a big company one may have a feeling of being isolated from the action, or not understanding how one's work actually fits into the work of the organization. This can be frustrating to someone who needs to see the results of his or her work first hand.

However, the size of the corporate giants may offer a greater variety of experiences to its lawyers. If someone is unhappy in one area, there are likely to be opportunities in another area.

If you want to travel, the multi-office corporation may provide an opportunity to do so, while the single office corporation would not. In fact, the large multinational corporations may provide one of the few opportunities to enter the international law field. Many students express interest in practicing international law, unaware that international law is practiced in a relatively small number of companies and law firms. Because working in a foreign country is perceived by many as glamorous, this is an area that is frequently mentioned as a possible career by persons interested in law school. In many cases, the overseas jobs go to experienced attorneys while the younger lawyers do their "international practice" in law libraries in domestic law offices.

Although one out of ten practicing lawyers works for a corporation, corporate practice has not always been perceived as the most desirable career alternative. This perception was not at all fair to the corporations because, as it has been shown in this chapter, there are many possibilities in the field, and the challenge and benefits are at least comparable to those in private practice. One reason for this situation was that until recently many corporations hired only experienced lawyers for their law departments. Many of these experienced lawyers had been in large law firms, and had failed to make partner. Another reason was that the corporate law departments were simply not large enough and well-developed enough to be able to provide training to inexperienced attorneys.

In the past decade the face of the average corporate law department has changed dramatically. While many corporations still farm out a great deal of litigation, more and more of the legal work of the corporation is handled in-house. The primary explanation given for this change is cost. A private law firm will frequently charge $100/hour or more for its services, while the same work handled in-house will cost less that $50/hour. In addition, corporations have found that their own lawyers are closer to problems that arise than private law firms they might hire. The maze of federal, state and local laws and regulations, the need for on-the-spot response to problems and the advantage of having a lawyer with no other loyalties all contribute to making the in-house lawyer increasingly indispensible to the corporation.

Thus, corporate law departments are growing rapidly. They have turned more and more to the law schools and inexperienced lawyers to meet their employee needs. As this has happened, the number of law students who have made corporate law practice their career choice has increased. One of the biggest changes in law practice over the next ten years will undoubtedly be the continued growth of the corporate field.

Overleaf: The Honorable Constance Baker Motley, Judge, U. S. District Court, Southern Dist. of New York, with Renee Jones Weeks, attorney and vice president of the NBA. Photo: National Bar Association.

CHAPTER 5

THE GOVERNMENT LAWYER

Charles had gone to work for the federal government as soon as he graduated from law school. His work with a large regulatory agency provided an outlet for his long expressed desire to help society. Another factor in his decision to go to Washington was 'Potomac fever,' and a longing to see more of the world than his home community.

The number of lawyers employed by the government at all levels has increased dramatically over the past half century. Beginning with the New Deal ushered in by President Franklin D. Roosevelt, the government has mushroomed as society attempted to solve a myriad of social problems through governmental action.

Politics aside, the rise of big government has paralleled the increase in the number of government lawyers. Although there have been those who have blamed lawyers for this growth, an understanding of the role of the lawyer should convince the observer that lawyers have acted primarily as the instruments of their clients in causing or reacting to this growth.

Lawyers serve in many positions in government. They work as counsel of administrative and regulatory agencies. This means that they must advise administrative officials in a wide variety of situations including the propriety or legality of their actions.

They do research and drafting, conduct quasi-judicial hearings, and go to court if required. Government lawyers in criminal cases prosecute defendants on behalf of the state, while in some cases the defense attorney is a government lawyer, too.

Many lawyers also perform administrative duties either in addition to or instead of working as lawyers in the agency. Lawyers work in every level of government; federal, state, and local, as well as international agencies such as the United Nations. This chapter deals with the major areas in which lawyers are employed. The number of government lawyers is somewhere between 12–13 percent of the bar. Their numbers have grown rapidly since 1950 when they comprised less than 10 percent of the bar, although the percentage seems to be leveling off now.

The opportunities with the federal government are as varied as the departments themselves, and the departments are as varied as the problems facing the country today. For almost every facet of American life there is a government agency designated to deal with it. Within this framework, the opportunities for employment are virtually endless. The diversity of activities within the broad scope of "government service" necessitates the careful investigation of each individual department, as each is a unique entity with its own particular advantages and disadvantages. A person who would not be at all interested in dealing with consumer protection law and anti-trust law with the Federal Trade Commission, or dealing with the problems of rural America via the Department of Agriculture, might find work with the Tax Division or the Justice Department to be the most ideal employment imaginable.

Government service offers opportunity for specialization. Although some would criticize government for its "bigness," in truth each department has a certain degree of autonomy and self-sufficiency. Federal government lawyers tend to work in departments with other lawyers who have the same expertise, whether it be admiralty, tax, transportation, communications, anti-trust, banking, patents, labor, or an almost infinite list of other possibilities. While many legal jobs are in the Washington, D.C. area, the existence of regional offices of many agencies provides federal legal jobs throughout the country. In addition, U.S. attorneys and federal public defender positions are available in every area.

For almost every federal agency, there are analogous agencies charged with similar responsibilities in every state. For law school graduates seeking employment with state agencies, the road to employment may seem filled with obstacles, and appear at times impassable. In many states there is no centralized organization or bureau which coordinates the hiring of personnel. Yet, despite this, it is possible to find the way to gainful employment.

In every state there is an office of the attorney general. The attorney general is responsible for defending the state when it is sued which, in this day and time, is frequently. The attorney general is also required to advise state officials on the legality of actions they might be considering. In recent years many aggressive attorneys general have attempted to enforce the rights of individual citizens or groups in such areas as consumer protection, environmental safety, and civil rights. Although the attorney general's office, as it is called, acts as the state's law firm and is usually the largest employer of attorneys in state government, there are attorneys in most agencies, and in fact, lawyers often hold many of the high administrative positions in those agencies. One area that is often overlooked as a career path for lawyers is education. Although teaching and administrative positions are dealt with in another chapter, it may be noteworthy that these lawyers often serve as general counsel for a school or college as an equal employment opportunity (EEO) officer, a labor lawyer, or any one of a number of other positions.

Jobs with governmental entities smaller than the state level are often hard to find because there are such a multitude of potential places to look. District, county, and city attorneys' offices quite often hire recent graduates. These offices are primarily thought of as prosecutors' offices because they represent the state in criminal cases. They may, however, have civil responsibilities representing a city or county government just as the attorney general represents the state. There are also many opportunities in fields such as land use planning or utilities law, in departments within city government, and in special districts (e.g., water, school, regional planning). Local government agencies, especially in smaller cities, are more likely to recruit from members of the local bar than to solicit applicants from law schools.

The Armed Forces are among the largest employers of lawyers in the country. To serve the legal needs of their personnel, the Army, Air Force, Navy, and Marine Corps have their Judge Advocate General's Corps or equivalent. The Army JAG Corps claims to be the world's largest law firm. In a period when jobs may be tight elsewhere, the salary, benefits, and relative security of military life may be attractive to many graduates. However, some legal employers outside the military system are reluctant to give full credit to experience gained in JAG.

When laypersons think of the judiciary, the image perceived is often of an elderly white haired man in a black robe sitting in a somber courtroom. There are thousands of judges in both federal and state courts. Many of these judges are quite young, only a few years out of college and law school, and not all of them are men. It is not an unreasonable expectation for someone to move up through the judicial system to increasingly higher courts. However, most judges are appointed to the bench after distinguished careers as practicing lawyers or educators. Because of the prestige associated with the position of judge an appointment or election (in jurisdictions where that is the method of judicial selection) is considered a badge of honor. The courts, through the conduct and performance of judges, can offer to the populace a sense of justice and confidence in an ordered society that few other individuals can ever hope to provide.

Court administrators are employees of the court who run the business of conducting court: setting the docket, notifying litigants of proceedings, directing court personnel, and managing the budget. Although it is not a prerequisite, many court administrators are lawyers who find the combination of business and high-level law satisfying.

An increasing number of students are taking advantage of opportunities to serve as clerks to federal or state judges. Those who have clerked almost always remember their one to two years of working for the judge with fondness, as a time of growth and learning, and often as an opportunity to develop a close relationship with another person.

A clerkship for the United States Court of Appeals or Supreme Court tends to involve less action and more scholarship than a clerkship for a federal district court. A major portion of an appellate clerk's time is consumed in research and writing. When a case comes to the Court of Appeals, most of the routine questions already have been ironed out in the district court, and the difficult questions are left for the appellate court to consider. Thus, the appellate clerk is afforded an opportunity to study fewer questions, but in more depth.

The range of legal problems encountered in a federal court of appeals is quite wide. A sampling would include *habeas corpus*, criminal law and procedure, labor, administrative procedure, tax, admiralty, anti-trust, securities, bankruptcy, civil rights, selective service, patents, poverty, social security, and welfare. In addition, because of the federal court's diversity jurisdiction, a federal court encounters the normal range of common law matters, including contracts, torts, and occasionally property matters. Of course, in connection with all the above cases, the court has the usual range of procedural and evidentiary questions.

There is an attractive opportunity to travel as a clerk for the Circuit Court. A clerk also participates in whatever three-judge court cases his judge is assigned to in the state in which the judge resides. The clerk always attends oral argument, and from this experience he learns a great deal about what to do, and what not to do, as a lawyer presenting a case orally to a judge.

While an appellate clerk does not have much direct contact with trial practice, he does have an opportunity to pick up a great deal of information about trial practice from his study of trial records which are always included in an appeal. He or she reads all the motions and pleadings filed in the trial court, and usually studies the trial transcript if there is one. This is valuable training in how to prepare a record for appeal.

The duties of a clerk for a federal district judge are somewhat different and quite varied. Most federal judges are prone to utilize a law clerk as a valuable adjunct to the judicial decision-making process. Law clerks will spend some time in the courtroom actually hearing the evidence and will advise, aid and assist the court in preparation of memorandum opinions or judgments.

There is much activity outside the courtroom in connection with pre-trial motions and memorandum opinions. It will be necessary for the law clerk to examine all of the pleadings and briefs and prepare memoranda for consideration by the judge. These memoranda will be studied by the judge and then active discussion will take place between the judge and the law clerk with a view to the positions taken by the respective parties and their merits.

A law clerk is a valuable sounding board, against whom can be "bounced" legal theories offered by the litigating parties, legal concepts overlooked by the parties, and the consequences of a decision to be rendered.

The position of a law clerk has the advantage of daily exposure to varied personality types. The law clerk will have the advantage of sitting in on conferences between the judge and the parties in connection with litigation in progress.

The exposure of a law clerk in a United States District Court runs the full gamut of all judicial proceedings entertained in these courts. The exposure includes civil and criminal matters, specialized matters such as admiralty, patent and bankruptcy litigation, and includes the opportunity to participate in *habeas corpus* proceedings or constitutional questions. The opportunity to become exposed to the members of the private bar in the cities in which court is held and to determine first hand their legal capabilities or weaknesses is a valuable experience. A law clerk also has an opportunity to work with the representatives of the Department of Justice and other government agencies in connection with their litigation in the U.S. courts.

A law clerk has an opportunity to learn from first-hand experience the procedural niceties of civil and criminal trials and to observe these matters "in action." A law clerk's experience becomes extremely valuable from the standpoint of future employment in the legal profession or with the government. Most law firms and government agencies desire experienced law clerks and reward their service.

Any person who desires to translate the academic approach of the classroom to the practical approach of the law in action can do himself a great service by undertaking an opportunity to serve as a judicial law clerk. After all, it is in court where the action is. It is there that the litigants face each other across the table and do legal battle before a judge and a jury.

State courts, like the federal courts, hire law graduates as law clerks. At the state level there are both trial and appellate courts, just as in the federal system. The duties of state appellate court clerks are very similar to those of clerks for the U.S. Court of Appeals. However, in many states trial court judges do not hire law clerks.

It should come as no surprise that lawyers are the most common occupational group represented among legislators. Until only a few years ago, they comprised the majority in many state legislatures. In fact, the terms lawyer and lawmaker are almost synonymous to many people. Unfortunately, this confusion is partly responsible for the low opinion some people have of the legal profession. Yet, there is a grain of truth there, because lawyers have traditionally been highly visible in the legislative branch of government. The drafting of laws quite often requires the mind of a lawyer to articulate the appropriate language. The persuasion needed to pass a law often requires the argumentative skill of a lawyer. And the compromising required to forge a law acceptable to a majority of the legislative body often requires the skill of a lawyer as negotiator.

Lawyers not only serve in the legislatures and Congress, they work on staffs as aides, fundraisers, researchers, speech writers, organizers, committee counsel and advisors. It is a rare politician—whether a lawyer himself or not—who is not surrounded by staff lawyers. How many Americans who watched the Watergate hearings can forget John Dean's famous "list of attorneys"? He started making a list of everyone he knew who could be indicted on criminal charges; and then checked off the attorneys, to discover that he had marked almost the entire list. It was a sad day for the profession and the country, but this incident is a constant reminder to those of us who are licensed attorneys that we have taken an oath to uphold the law and we can never forget the ethical requirements that go with that oath.

A final area of employment for lawyers in government is public administration. Included in this field are such things as policy analysis, program development, personnel management, and legislative work for an agency (what would be called lobbying in the private sector). Although these positions involve work which may be handled by non-lawyers, legal skills can be invaluable tools to persons employed in much of the public administration area.

Overleaf: Audience participation at the National Bar Association symposium on "Critical Title VII Issues" at the 53rd Annual NBA Convention, where the theme was, "Black Lawyers: Catalysts for Change." Photo: NBA.

CHAPTER 6

PRACTICE IN THE PUBLIC INTEREST

Carol, the intellectual of our group, and a product of academia, was totally at ease in the intellectual jousting tournament of law school. Carol's greatest asset was her profound grasp of deductive reasoning, which enabled her to fathom even the most complex issues. After graduation, Carol gravitated toward a career with a public interest law firm, where she researches and analyzes trend-setting litigation.

Legal aid and social services employment will not bring great wealth; in fact, it is even doubtful that it will bring great notoriety. One who chooses this path may face a heavy caseload and relentless adversity. The primary rewards are personal and these do not need to be enumerated. Those who enter this type of practice are in short supply. Those who do choose legal services can rest assured that they are genuinely needed.

The Western Center on Law & Poverty has published a brochure in which they state their concept of the need for people in poverty law: "We say we are a nation of laws, not of men. But men make the laws, interpret them, administer them, proclaim them, and enforce them. It is not the law which fails; but people who fail to make it apply equally to all.

"Too often the poor have viewed the law as a technicality, an obstruction, something that takes away their freedom, limits their existence, proscribes their behavior, puts them down. They have not seen it as a champion of their rights. The Legal Services program has taken the position that the poor have the same rights as the rich and that they are entitled to the same high quality legal counsel. This sentiment is commendable, but it ranks low in the order of the nation's priorities."

Legal services programs seek to provide representation to persons and groups who could not otherwise afford it. The category includes legal aid and public defender work, as well as the broad area of law reform. Not all legal services programs are involved in all these areas. Funding comes primarily from governmental and private foundation sources. Because ethnic and racial minorities constitute an inordinate percentage of the poor, minority lawyers who can communicate effectively with these clients are greatly needed.

What does a legal services attorney do? Most non-lawyers as well as many lawyers would be hard-pressed to tell. The image of an overworked and underpaid gladiator comes readily to mind. They are overworked because even at present levels of support, less than 30% of the legal needs of the poor in this country are currently being met. There is literally no end to the work to be done. They are underpaid in that their salaries are among the lowest in the legal profession for lawyers of comparable experience and ability. The reasons for this are threefold. First, it is difficult to justify high salaries for attorneys whose clients have no money. Second, critical choices have to be made by program administrators, and they frequently elect to fund more positions at lower salaries, than to pay more money to fewer lawyers. Third, individuals who seek legal services careers are usually motivated by factors other than money.

Funding for legal services programs comes through the Congress for the 320 programs of the Legal Services Corporation, although some programs are funded by state, local, and private sources as well. Funding is never enough.

The turnover in legal services jobs is probably highest in the profession. While the level of personal satisfaction may be very high, the frustration level can be higher. Like many other high stress occupations, like ambulance drivers, air traffic controllers, school teachers, and placement directors, legal aid attorneys often begin to lose motivation and effectiveness after a few years of continually facing adversity with little hope of respite.

Disillusionment can also be a cause for turnover among younger attorneys. Many a recent graduate with high ideals has become discouraged when faced with the reality of dealing with poverty and its seamy effects. This "save the world" syndrome can be shattered very quickly by the sight of a welfare mother with nine starving children who has come for help because her landlord has legally evicted her.

Poor people have more problems than people of means. They are statistically less educated and so they have more difficulty fending for themselves in the world of business and commerce. They are easily "ripped off." They have fewer clothes. They eat less. They are sick more. Their problems keep them out of good jobs that could free them from their unfortunate status.

Their legal problems grow out of their condition. They are hopelessly outmatched in the legal arena without the help of a competent attorney, but turnover in the ranks of the legal aid attorneys diminishes the effectiveness of the program.

This may sound pessimistic to some and may discourage young lawyers from entering this field. It is not meant to be so. It is meant rather to tell people the truth about what to expect. Good people committed to working for the poor are needed. It is important, however, to strip away the gloss that is sometimes put upon legal services work by its fervent advocates. If this picture is not overwhelming, if you still find the idea of public interest practice appealing, then you should pursue a career in this area with vigor.

In many ways legal aid lawyers are like other lawyers. They

have law offices, secretaries and paralegals. They interview clients, do research in the library, prepare legal documents and go to court. They work hard. They strive to negotiate the best possible deal for their clients. Their offices may not be quite as fancy, they may be motivated more by altruistic than profit motives, and they may drive a VW Rabbit instead of a BMW, but the skills they must use to be successful are the very same as those required to be successful as a corporate lawyer, a government lawyer, or a private practitioner.

The areas of law most commonly practiced in legal aid are domestic relations, landlord-tenant law, consumer protection law, debtor-creditor law, and civil rights law. Criminal law is not included because criminal practice is usually practiced in the public defenders' office, although much of what has been said about the civil legal aid lawyer could be said about the public defender too.

Because of the turnover problem mentioned previously, there are many opportunities in the legal services field. In addition, the interest in public service jobs has dropped since the late 60s and early 70s when a high percentage of law students entered law school because they "wanted to help make the world a better place to live." However, the availability of positions is uneven. In the larger cities where a larger number of graduates settle jobs are harder to find, especially where the local legal aid program maintains some form of clinical or internship program with local law schools. Moreover, the movement of experienced lawyers into the cities will make it difficult for inexperienced attorneys to find jobs. The avenue for many young lawyers in the 80s may be to begin their careers on the staffs of rural legal aid programs in less desirable areas. With the exception of a few post graduate fellowships such as the Regmalel Heber Smith Community Lawyer Fellowship Program, most of the attractive jobs in the legal services as well as in the public interest field go to lawyers who have paid their dues, or developed credentials in the field through actual practice. Aspiring public interest lawyers would be wise to begin even before law school to do community service work even on a volunteer basis.

The theme of this chapter is that there is a need for lawyers who serve people with low incomes. There are many difficulties and frustrations. The situation may be unsatisfactory in many ways but the rewards are clearly there for those who are willing to make the commitment.

The question is, are you willing to sacrifice a lucrative position in private practice for the satisfaction of doing something that must be done? It is eventually a question of ordering priorities in an effort to determine what it is that you want from your profession. Your profession is one that has prepared you for such a vast range of service that the decision is an extremely difficult one. In the past few years, there has been an ever increasing sensitivity to the problems of poor and minority individuals. Along with this awareness has come a desire, on the part of many, to help make the vital changes which must take place if justice is to be a reality.

As a lawyer you may have the opportunity, at least in some way, to bring about change, but dedication to the social services involves some sacrifice in terms of personal comforts. However, if you feel that you could not be satisfied with anything short of complete involvement in these problems, perhaps social services and law reform is the area of law which you would find most rewarding. The degree to which you dedicate yourself to solving these problems could range from an entire career devoted to legal aid, to occasional *pro bono* (Latin: *pro bono publico*: for the public good) work while engaged in private practice.

Citizens in the United States have in recent years begun to view the law as a vehicle for promoting the public interest instead of as a tool of special interests. Or one could say that new special interests have evolved to represent groups which have not tended to use the judicial system to protect their rights in the past. No matter which view one takes, the fact remains that more people than ever before are getting involved in the legal process.

Some of the areas that have aroused considerable interest are consumer protection, environmental law and land use planning, communications, and governmental responsiveness and ethics. Whenever a group of concerned citizens attempts to assert or defend its rights, lawyers are likely to be involved.

Funding for public interest representation has come to a certain extent through the government and charitable sources, but a large part of the burden has been shouldered by the citizens who are represented. These groups are very often neither very rich nor very poor. Things like PIRGs (public interest research groups), prepaid legal service plans, and citizens' committees are usually paid for by those who reap the benefits.

Just as in legal services law, public interest law may involve legal advice and representation for law reform. Groups may secure someone in a law firm to represent them, they may hire a staff counsel, or they may rely on volunteers to handle their legal work. Lack of government support, tighter foundation budgets, and economic woes on the part of ordinary citizens have made good-paying jobs in the public interest field scarce and competition fierce. But for persons willing to make the commitment, the need is there. It is exciting to view the significant numbers of good law students that are finding the problems impossible to ignore.

This interest in public interest or *pro bono* work has extended beyond the law schools and law students to the organized bar itself. There is an ongoing debate today on the nature and extent of the individual lawyer's responsibility to society to perform *pro bono* work. Is the lawyer's only responsibility to the client? Can the lawyer's own monetary concerns stand before obligations to society? Can the bar or another agency enforce such an obligation? Who is to decide what is in the public interest if not the lawyer? These questions are not easy ones, but they are questions that every lawyer, every law student, and every person planning a career in law should consider.

Overleaf: The old part of Townes Hall, the Law School Building, University of Texas at Austin. Photo: Frank Armstrong.

CHAPTER 7

LAWYERS IN ACADEMIA

John, a West Point graduate who had become
an outspoken critic of the Vietnam War and now,
as a public interest lawyer, was so persuasive that
he was hired by a major university as their lobbyist.
Just when everyone thought that John had 'arrived'
at the pinnacle of his career, he quit his job to go
back to school for his L.L.M., a graduate law degree.

Law school teaching tends to be very exclusive and entry into
the profession, difficult. Although this varies from school to
school, most entrants into teaching among recent graduates
were law review editors, number one grads, U.S. Supreme Court
clerks, and the like. For those not so fortunate as to possess these
credentials there are two basic ways to find a position.

The first is to develop expertise and/or recognition in some
field and to be considered a leader in that field. This recognition
typically takes ten years or so to gain, but occasionally may take
less.

The second approach is to do graduate work at a school which
has a program oriented toward teacher training. The better programs have seminars in teaching law, and students have the opportunity to continue to write and develop in their professional
areas. Many law schools use advanced degree candidates to teach
the legal research courses, either for direct pay or fellowships.

Teaching legal subjects has gone far beyond just teaching in law schools. Universities, colleges, and community and junior colleges are showing a great increase in law-related courses like Business Law, Individual Rights, Paralegal Training, Law Enforcement, and others. Some individuals find jobs by applying to the colleges as teachers of these new legal subjects.

Various professional associations in the academic world handle recruitment of new teachers in their area just as the Association of American Law Schools (AALS) does in law. These associations should be contacted directly by those interested in a particular specialty. In addition, the *Chronicle of Higher Education* lists job openings in the general teaching field.

Many lawyers assume responsibilities in the areas of educational administration, student personnel administration, financial aid, placement, admissions, and legal advising for school districts, colleges, and universities, as well as law schools.

The administrator is called upon almost daily to deal with legal questions. In areas such as equal employment opportunity, educational rights and privacy, and countless others, legal training is invaluable.

Law librarianship is a job that combines the satisfaction of a research and planning career with the excitement inherent in working with the legal profession. Continuing accumulation of court decisions, rapid expansion of government regulation at all levels, and new legal problems caused by social change have produced a need for specialization in the practice and knowledge of law and management of the materials that are the lawyer's tools. Computer science is having an impact upon libraries in both management and research aspects of library service. Law librarians serve the legal profession in courts, bar associations, law schools, international agencies, law firms, government offices, and businesses.

Legal research, editing, and publishing is an interesting field which many law students do not consider. Qualified editors are in short supply and there are many legal publishers and research organizations. The influence of computerized legal research is having an impact on employers in both areas. While research and editing require a special kind of person, many law graduates will find just what they are looking for in this field.

Some students who have a law degree believe that further education is important for their career plans. Combining different degrees may qualify a lawyer for jobs in a second area of training and may provide greater opportunity, but it may also lead to the risk of over-qualification.

There are also a number of post-graduate fellowships available. Some of these are well-known and others less recognized. The competition for all is stiff but the benefits can be great.

White House Fellowships: the purpose of the program is to give the Fellows first-hand, high-level experience with the workings of the federal government and to increase their sense of participation in national affairs.

The Fellows are younger men and women, age 23 to 35, chosen from business, law, journalism, the universities, architecture, or other occupations. Each has demonstrated high moral character, exceptional ability, marked leadership qualities, and the unusual promise of future development.

There are 15 White House Fellows each year and they serve for 15 months. One Fellow is assigned to the office of the Vice-President; one to each Cabinet officer; and four to members of the White House staff. In addition to their daily work, the Fellows take part in seminars and other activities especially planned to advance the purposes of the program.

The Fellows are named by the President on the recommendation of a Commission on White House Fellows. All inquiries and requests for application blanks should be addressed to the Director, Commission on White House Fellows, The White House, Washington, D.C.

Fulbright Scholarships: The U. S. Government Scholarships

for Graduate Study Abroad, established under the Fulbright-Hays Act, are awarded each year to American citizens who will hold a bachelor's degree or its equivalent before the beginning of the grant. The students must know the languages of the countries in which they wish to study—well enough to carry on study and reasearch. Recipients are selected on the basis of personal qualifications, academic record, and the value of the study or project they have proposed.

Where qualifications are otherwise equal, veterans and persons under 35 years of age receive preference. Any qualified American citizen at home or abroad may apply but, as a general policy, preference is given to applicants who have not previously lived or studied abroad. Students receiving grants are assisted by the United States Educational Foundation Commission abroad in obtaining admission to a foreign educational institution. Awards are made in the currencies of participating countries and ordinarily cover living expenses, transportation, tuition, books, and/or equipment for one academic year. The terms of the Fulbright-Hays Act require affiliation with an educational institution. This competition also includes travel grants for students holding scholarships from other sources, and English Language Teaching Grants in certain foreign countries.

IIE Foreign Fellowships: These provide foreign study and research opportunities, mainly in Europe, offered by foreign governments, universities, and private donors. These are administered by the Institute of International Education, 809 United Nations Plaza, New York, NY 10017.

Marshall Scholarships: these may be used at any university in the United Kingdom for a period of two years but may be extended for a third year. Marshall Scholars are required to enroll as degree candidates at a British University. Candidates must be U.S. citizens, under 26 on October 1st of the year in which awards are taken up. In exceptional cases, candidates up to the age of 28 may be considered.

Overleaf: Law school students may develop interests in related, but non-legal careers such as management, judicial administration, law enforcement, and many others. Photo: University of Texas Law School.

CHAPTER 8

LAWYERS IN OTHER CAREERS

Ted could best be called an entrepreneur. A century earlier, Ted might have made his fortune peddling snake oil or magic elixir. During law school and for the first couple of years thereafter, he created a consumer research organization and persuaded literally thousands of people to join his cause. Then he went into the magazine business.

Many law students either do not want to practice law upon graduation or have serious questions as to whether they would really enjoy doing so, although the great majority of law students do seek legally related jobs.

This section attempts to do two things: to define which jobs are law-related or non-legal, and to suggest ways of approaching the job market in these areas. Students are urged to consider non-legal jobs only if they, after having made a careful self-analysis, really want to go that route. By the same token, students should not refrain from considering non-legal employment if they think they might like it just because a majority of their classmates choose law careers.

"Law-related and non-legal" could refer to almost any occupation from garbage collection to corporate management. There are thousands of job titles recognized by the Bureau of Labor Statistics. Therefore, when we refer to "non-legal" jobs, we mean positions other than law practice where law graduates would have a distinct advantage over other applicants, or where knowledge of the law would prove to be a valuable asset on the job. Often pre-legal training combined with a legal education will provide special qualifications in young attorneys. Where it appears that additional training and/or experience would be especially worthwhile or necessary, students should not hesitate to obtain these qualifications.

The number of careers open to legally trained persons is extensive. There are legal considerations in every form of human endeavor in this complex world. Even when not "practicing law" in the sense of giving legal advice to clients, a lawyer working in a field other than law will be dealing with the interface between law and that field. It is arguable that legal skills give the lawyer a much better ability to manage this interface than the non-lawyer. In a broader sense it is probably true that legal skills such as spotting issues, analyzing problems, conducting research, and persuading others can be useful in almost every job.

LAW–RELATED OPTIONS

Lawyers whose activities do not constitute practicing law are often described as working in non-traditional or alternative careers. Such terminology is unfortunate because it implies that such positions are second rate. It makes more sense to describe the non-legal and law-related work simply as "options."

It is beyond the scope of this chapter to describe in detail all the career options available to attorneys. The recent NALP Employment Survey for the Class of 1978 identified 105 different non-legal jobs accepted by law graduates. The opportunities described are just as real for the career changer as for the recent graduate. Those who wonder if law practice will be satisfying for them should ask themselves the question: "Can my skills be better used in a different field?" If so, it might be time to consider something other than one of the traditional areas of law practice.

Non-legal positions for lawyers may be found in a variety of organizational settings. Many are in business and industry, at all levels of the corporate structure. Many are in government—federal, state, local, and multinational agencies. Some are in quasi-governmental private associations or corporations. Many positions are in institutions including professional organizations, and in educational institutions, both public and private. In some instances, the jobs discussed will be found in only one area such as corporate; in others, they will be found in different organizational settings.

Administration and Management

The first group of jobs are those in the business administration and management areas. These positions may be found in corporations, in government at all levels, and in private associations. In large corporate concerns, there are often formal in-house training programs. However, the real trend in business today is for the small business to hire a lawyer/manager. Organizations attempting to reduce skyrocketing legal expenses, but not large enough to consider developing an in-house legal department, often seek lawyers with some business experience to fill management positions with limited "legal advisor" functions. Industrial companies, banks, insurance companies, and other businesses will consider legally trained individuals who have a background in or demonstrate a facility for managerial work. Management or public administration positions in government are often filled by lawyers as are management positions and directorships of many private associations. This group includes bar associations and law firms.

Money Management

When one thinks of money management, banks and accounting firms come to mind. Commercial banking and public accounting have attracted many qualified lawyers over the years. Accounting firms frequently recruit alongside law firms at law schools although partnerships in public accounting firms are restricted to holders of the CPA certificate. However, it is possible to complete the CPA requirements after graduating from school. Banks frequently hire lawyers to work in the trust department although some banks use lawyers in the commercial banking area. Brokerage houses and investment firms have been known to employ lawyers, but this is a less common practice than with banks and accounting firms. Fund-raising positions, which often involve coordinating deferred giving programs, are filled from time to time with lawyers, especially those with experience in estate or trust work. Fund-raising may take place in the corporation, the educational institution, the private foundation, or the political arena.

Planning and Organization

Planners are found everywhere, although it is not always possible to tell where they have been after they have left. The fields of systems analysis and professional consulting call for considerable expertise in the substantive professional area, and the legal problems faced by planners attempting to integrate new technology into existing systems make legally trained persons valuable in this area. While many planning positions are in the public sector, there are opportunities in the private sector as well.

Insurance

Insurance is mentioned as a separate category because it is such a large industry. Positions for lawyers outside the general counsel's office are basically in three areas: sales, plan management, and claims adjustment. Insurance sales can be lucrative work, but it is not for everyone. A number of insurance companies recruit attorneys for positions as sales representatives to handle complex benefit plans and insurance programs for corporations, partnerships, and professionals. Plan management is a term intended to describe everything done by the insurance company in its home office or branch offices to administer its accounts. Claims adjustment positions have in the past provided limited opportunities for lawyers, although claims work can be a stepping stone to other opportunities in the company.

Administration of Justice

The judicial system from the non-lawyer's perspective is comprised mainly of lawyers and judges. However, there are a great many opportunities for lawyers who do not practice law in the justice system. Judicial administration includes court administration—such positions as permanent court clerks, administrators, and court reporters. It also includes the broader area of criminal justice administration, and there are lawyers involved at almost every level in positions other than as advocates. Fields like prison or parole administration may require other specialized training than provided by law school, but fields such as law enforcement do not. Many police departments use in-house legal advisors who educate officers on legal issues. Some law graduates go into law enforcement as officers or agents (e.g., the FBI). There is also the area of private investigation, and some find it more exciting and rewarding to be Paul Drake than Perry Mason.

Real Estate

Many lawyers enter real estate after years of practicing law when they realize that their clients are making all the money. Some make the change gradually, others just quit their law practices. Real estate sales and development are two visible fields. Both represent very risky, highly competitive, but potentially highly lucrative careers. Less visible are the title companies. It is ironic that in many states practicing lawyers have complained that title companies have stolen their business, and now title insurance companies are being taken over by lawyers. Another area of growth in a world of limited energy is mineral land management and petroleum land management.

Legislation

More legislators come from law backgrounds than from any other professional group. The same is true of their aides, researchers, and paid campaigners. Many former legislators and lawyers become involved in lobbying for the multitude of organizations trying to influence legislation. Need more be said?

Communications

The skills of lawyering (writing, speaking, persuading) are the same skills required of individuals in the communications field. Some of the areas where lawyers have been successful are writing, publishing, broadcast and print journalism, acting, filmmaking, advertising, and public relations. While communications careers are attractive to many people, the opportunities are limited and a strong background in the communications field or personal contacts plus some good luck will undoubtedly be necessary for one to "break in."

Education

As mentioned previously there are opportunities for lawyers in education and education-related pursuits. Educational positions are not likely to be high-paying, but the freedom and creativity fostered in the educational setting combine to produce a strong attraction to many lawyers. Teaching positions are available in law schools, universities, community colleges, and secondary schools. Administrators, who may or may not be teachers, are involved in varied responsibilities throughout the academic environment. One growing field of work is in continuing legal education (CLE). The CLE field has grown dramatically in the last ten years with nearly every law school and bar association, as well as many private organizations, getting into the act. If mandatory CLE ever becomes a reality throughout the nation, CLE jobs will become even more common.

Many legal librarianships, research positions, and publishing jobs exist outside law schools and the traditional legal profession. These professional research groups and publishers as well as the educational institutions hire annually, although lawyers may not always work for them.

The Entrepreneurs

A discussion of alternatives would not be complete without mentioning the entrepreneurs. There are countless stories of lawyers who have founded businesses of their own and succeeded. Perhaps it is the tradition of hanging out a shingle or the independent nature of many who choose to go to law school. Perhaps it is the recognition of opportunities or contacts made during years of practicing law. Whatever the reasons, there are enough lawyers who strike out in business on their own that the possibility should be mentioned to potential career changers.

MANY ALTERNATIVES

This has been a quick overview of some of the careers pursued by lawyers who do *not* practice law. It should be remembered that all these jobs will not appeal to everyone. Moreover, this list is not intended to be inclusive of all the kinds of work that lawyers perform. The objective has been to suggest options for the student who, for whatever reasons, does not want to practice law. These options are not second-rate occupations; people who work in these areas generally do so because they want to and not because they have to. Non-legal jobs provide a future for members of the legal profession who are revolting against the conventional practice of law.

Overleaf: Randolph T. Blackwell, former director of the Office of Minority Business Enterprise, U. S. Department of Commerce, (left) Received the NBA Equal Justice Award from NBA President Mark T. McDonald at the 53rd Annual Convention.

CHAPTER 9

SUBSTANTIVE AREAS OF PRACTICE

Bill was in private practice with a small firm after law school. In his firm, the lawyers didn't specialize, but handled whatever walked through the door. No two days were the same, and the pressure was tremendous. Bill always took the burden of each client's problem upon himself, and there were numerous clients.

In previous chapters, the discussion has centered around the kind of organization in which law is practiced. There were law firms, corporations, agencies, private associations, and educational institutions, as well as numerous subcategories. These organizations all represent different clients, and the differences in how they practice often depend on whom they represent. The large firm is large in part because it represents large corporate clients with legal needs requiring a large number of lawyers.

Another way of looking at legal jobs is by looking at substantive areas of practice. An area of practice may be defined in terms of its substance or subject matter. A lawyer may be engaged in a certain substantive area of practice in any of a number of organizational settings. Some substantive areas require specialized training or education. However, an understanding of what kind of law is practiced should be useful to most pre-law students in planning their careers.

This chapter covers only a limited number of areas of practice and the reader should not think that the list is complete. In fact, almost every form of human endeavor has legal ramifications, and so the list could be much longer than it is. Because the world is changing, the areas of practice are always changing too. It is also worth noting that recent court decisions have opened the door to advertising by lawyers and to reductions in anti-competitive forms of practice. Non-lawyers now perform many tasks which were previously handled only by attorneys. The result of all this is that the line between what constitutes practicing law and what is not practicing law has become somewhat blurred. In years to come, historians may decide that the advertising issue was the key which opened the profession to its most revolutionary changes.

The areas listed here include many of the substantive areas of law being practiced today. There is a short description of each one. The reader is urged to refer to the bibliography for further reading.

BUSINESS AND CORPORATE LAW

This general heading refers to legal work that is performed for corporations. Corporations, from their creation to their dissolution, have a great many needs for legal counsel. While the majority of the corporations in the United States are still small "mom and pop" operations that may use few attorneys, major companies require literally armies of them. On the whole, corporations require more legal work that the general population does. The fact that most corporate headquarters are in major cities results in much lower ratios of population-to-attorneys than in other cities. Some of the major categories of business and corporate work include:

General Business

This is a catch-all for any work that a business may encounter that is not included in any of the specialized areas described below. It may involve such diverse problems as white-collar crime or property acquisition

Securities

Securities work involves organizing and financing corporations. The lawyer's role in this process may involve preparing all the legal documents required in some very complex transactions, or coordinating transactions between the various parties with diverse interests that must reach agreement. Traditionally, securities work consisted largely of corporate formations. In recent years, more and more of the work has involved mergers and acquisitions or corporate takeovers. A lawyer may also work in the area of organizing smaller business entities such as partnerships and professional or closely held corporations that do not involve stock registrations. In some areas, such as health care, law firms have become highly specialized.

Taxation

One of the most complex areas of law is tax law. Just like the individual taxpayer, the corporation wants to give as little to the government as legally possible. The word *legally* above is crucial, because this is what distinguishes tax law from the tax work of an accounting firm.

Many tax lawyers have accounting degrees and some are certified public accountants. A growing area of tax law is that having to do with pensions, benefits, and profit-sharing plans. Tax lawyers are kept busy by the periodic tax reform acts which change the existing laws in some way. When this happens (for instance, in the pension plan area) every business that is potentially affected will have to have legal help to review its procedures.

Contracts

This large area covers the buying and selling of goods and services and the formation of agreements among parties in the process.

Labor Relations

Labor law involves the relationship between a company and its employees, individually or as members of a union. Traditionally, labor law included application of the National Labor Relations Act and other labor legislation. In recent years, other areas such as employment discrimination have grown in importance to the practice.

Antitrust Problems

A final area of corporate practice is the antritust field. Since the enactment of the Sherman Antitrust Act, corporations have been prohibited from taking actions which would result in the reduction or elimination of competition in the free market. Monopolistic practices of large companies are often the subject of suits by smaller ones. These suits pitting corporation against corporation can be complex, lengthy, and expensive. A suit against IBM by several smaller firms has been in litigation for 20 years. The stakes in these suits may run into hundreds of millions of dollars.

Government Relations

More and more companies are allocating large sums of money to government relations, including lobbying and drafting legislation, and helping the company to wade through a sea of governmental regulation.

SERVICES FOR INDIVIDUAL CLIENTS

Traditional legal work outside the business world includes a number of areas performed by lawyers for individual clients.

Real Estate

This is the buying and selling, renting and leasing of land, usually including buildings. While commercial real estate should perhaps be included under business law, by far the larger segment of real estate practice involves land transactions by people who own private property.

Domestic Relations

Domestic relations or family law deals with legal problems of marital or family relationships. Divorce is a common legal action included under family law, although adoption, guardianship, custody, and other familial relationships should not be overlooked. The domestic relations lawyer must be an effective counselor because of the highly emotional nature of his or her work.

Wills and Estates

The transfer of property after a property holder's death is one of the oldest functions of lawyers. In ancient times, the power to dispose of the family wealth was one of the most important functions of the family head. Through the will, the deceased person could determine the division of his (or her) property. In twentieth century America, tax considerations may be as critical to estate planning as disposition of the assets of the estate.

Tort Law

Tort law includes both personal injury law and a variety of administrative remedies such as workers compensation. In the personal injury area, most of the work involves litigation and lawyers tend to be rather rigidly divided according to whom they represent. There are the plaintiffs lawyers and there are the defense lawyers.

Criminal Law

As long as civilization attempts to punish criminal behavior, there will be criminal lawyers, both prosecutors and defense lawyers. To many people, the Perry Mason type of criminal lawyer is what they picture when they think of a lawyer. While criminal law is a large area of practice it is only a small part of the legal profession.

Litigation

Some of the work already described may be included under the heading litigation. Litigation is the work that a lawyer performs in the courtroom. There is both trial work and appellate work. Trial lawyers are often perceived as hard driving, aggressive individuals who are never at a loss for words. The key to successful litigation is preparation and not necessarily aggressiveness. Many of the finest trial lawyers are mild-mannered individuals.

MUNICIPAL LAW

Municipal law, as the name suggests, is the law dealing with municipalities—cities and other local governmental bodies. Municipal law includes such matters as zoning, condemnation, taxation of property, municipal bonds, and the great number of laws governing the conduct of citizens of the city. As advisor to the city government, the municipal lawyer must be a constitutional lawyer. He or she advises on the constitutionality of ordinances and must draft ordinances that can be upheld in court as constitutional. As a representative of the people, the municipal lawyer must prosecute those who violate the law. In some cities this is handled by a special criminal district attorney office. In other cities some or all of the prosecution is performed by the city attorney.

PUBLIC UTILITIES LAW

In recent years, one of the most significant areas of practice is public utilities law. This may include everything from telephone service, to water and sewage, to power. With the energy crisis, limited resources, and skyrocketing costs, the challenges facing the utilities lawyer are spectacular.

ENERGY LAW

Energy law is likely to be the most important area of practice, and unquestionably the area of greatest growth, in the next 25 years. Energy law involves rights to resources and their sale. In the case of coal, oil, gas, and other minerals, it is the rights to the resources in the earth. New developments in energy law have touched upon questions about legal rights to use sun, wind, and water power.

Energy law involves the rights to produce, distribute, and sell energy which has been developed. It also involves the dangers involved in the production of energy, including environmental pollution, problems with safety of nuclear power, land use rights and, increasingly, air use rights. Energy law involves transportation, taxation, and patents needed in the research and development process. By virtue of its pervasiveness, energy involves governmental regulation.

PATENT AND COPYRIGHT LAW

Patent law is a highly specialized field which involves protecting the right of inventors to the profits they may be able to gain from their inventions. The patent lawyer almost always possesses, in addition to a law degree, a degree in engineering or a technical scientific field, since understanding the technical side of inventions is as important as understanding the law. Patent law is frequently grouped with copyright law under the broad heading *intellectual property law.* Authors and artists receive protection for their creations and the profits they may make from them just as inventors do.

ENTERTAINMENT LAW

One area where copyright law is especially critical is entertainment law. Writers, composers, arrangers and other artists' work is protected by law. Entertainment law also involves contracts among artists, promoters, and distributors. It includes the business affairs of all sorts of entertainers: movie, theater, and television actors, lecturers, musicians, singers, dancers, painters, and professional athletes.

EDUCATION LAW

Education law is also an area of growing importance. Public school districts, private schools, colleges and universities are more than ever in the public eye. Rights of students to privacy and rights of access to records have become issues in recent years. The role of schools as institutions responsible for students is currently at issue. Funding is a never-ending problem. Students' rights, teachers' rights, and faculty rights frequently conflict, and as never before the average citizen wants to be involved in the educational process, as well.

EMERGING AREAS OF LAW

There are other areas where a militant public has literally created whole new areas of law; or at least it can be said that public involvement has brought legal questions in many areas to prominence. Environmental problems, consumer rights, malpractice by professionals, truth in lending and advertising, and water use rights, health care, and occupational health and safety are all areas of law taking on new importance.

The emergence of these "new" fields of practice suggests the dynamic nature of law and law practice. It is never static and always changing. The problems of today may be supplanted by others tomorrow. This discussion of substantive areas of law practice barely scratches the surface of possibilities.

A closing example will illustrate how an area of practice can change in a relatively short time. For years, the immigration of aliens into the United States was strictly regulated and the flow quite small. Immigration law was once a very narrow field. Then things began to change. The economic growth of the American border states began to attract an increasing number of Mexicans to work in this country. Some came legally; many more came illegally, often encouraged by organizations that made a business of transporting the people illegally over the border. The Mexican workers usually began as farmworkers, then became factory workers and office workers as they settled permanently. Illegal aliens who could be deported seldom were because they would work at a fraction of the pay of American workers. The aliens moved gradually but inevitably into the northern industrial centers. They were joined by thousands of Vietnamese in 1975 and thousands of Cubans in 1980. Suddenly, immigration law was no small business. What was to happen to these people? To their families? To their children born on American soil? To the American workers they displace? To the American employers who hire them? To the many others who interact with them? The legal problems that are emerging from the presence of these millions of people may take decades to untangle. Without making value judgments about such migration, it is safe to say that the world is much more complex than it was when immigrants from Europe poured into the United States in the 19th century. Immigration lawyers now deal with much more than naturalization. They handle labor law, criminal law, education and family law. All this could not have been predicted even twenty years ago. The future of this area of law is not easy to guess. Lawyers are the problem-solvers of our society. Whenever the issues become too complex to handle by self-help or government help, we turn to the law and the courts. If you want to find out what lawyers do, look around. Wherever you see people with legal relationships to define and legal problems to solve, you will inevitably find lawyers.

There are many other types of law not mentioned in this chapter. The list could go on and on. However, what has been covered here should give you an idea of the variety of substantive areas of practice available in a legal career.

Overleaf: Location and climate may be factors in selection of a law school. Photos: top, Gonzaga School of Law, Spokane, WA; bottom, Baylor University Law School, Waco, Texas. Photographer, above, Don H. Evavold.

CHAPTER 10

GETTING INTO LAW SCHOOL

Sam had elected to enter practice in a predominately black community. Sam had become a college debater in the South at a time when educational opportunities for blacks were less than spectacular. The year after graduation he accepted a fellowship with a national civil rights organization. His practice today, while quite broad, still maintains its civil rights flavor.

Most books on legal careers dwell interminably on getting into and going to law school. This one does not, because, as the title *Opportunities in Law Careers* suggests, careers are at the other end of the line. If the reader finds that a law career is not suited to him or her, that person should not go to law school. Law school is not the place to discover oneself.

Law school is a long and tortuous journey. Most people find it is the most demanding educational setting they have ever experienced. They must read more; they are challenged more; they are wrong more. Competition is intense. Law school is not a place for the faint-hearted or the uncommitted.

Law school is for people who want to be lawyers. Since there are so many areas where legal training is a useful or necessary background, a person has not narrowed the field irrevocably by choosing law. Still, some hard choices have to be made before ever coming to law school. Many law students who have come to law school confused about what they want to do with their lives have left it even more so.

For those who are unsure about their career goals, high school and college career counselors can be helpful. Work experience outside of school can also be useful. Many people today are electing to work for several years before applying to law school. This not only gives them time to examine their career plans, but also permits them to save money that will be needed to pay for a legal education. Furthermore, law students who have worked in the "real" world with its many demands often find the transition to law school less painful than the student who has gone straight through college without a break and is really tired of going to school.

The competition for admission to law school puts a heavy burden on the college pre-law student. There is a certain pressure to perform well academically throughout the college years. There is little room for mistakes such as one blown semester, a wrong choice of major, a year or two of too much play. While law school admissions committees may look behind a paper record and take into consideration bad semesters, each time you stumble you lessen your chances of eventually being admitted to law school. This may sound harsh, and perhaps it is. The purpose of this book is to present the truth and not a fairy tale. Even with a projected decrease in applications there will still be more candidates than accepted applicants.

Law school applicants often ask, "Does it make any difference where I went to school or what my major is?" The answer is not simple. Some schools admit students "by the numbers" usually a combination of undergraduate grade point average (GPA) and the Law School Admission Test (LSAT) scores. Other schools look at a number of other factors.

THE LSAT

The LSAT is a standardized test taken by all prospective law students. While it is possible to draw parallels between the LSAT and other standardized tests such as the SAT, GRE, and GMAT, the LSAT is specifically designed to predict law school success, by testing such skills as analyzing problems.

The predictive value of the LSAT has been questioned. Some schools claim a high correlation between LSAT score and first year law school grades. However, there are unresolved questions as to whether the test is culturally biased in favor of middle-class Anglo test takers and against minority ethnic groups. Furthermore some of those who take the test will do poorly on standardized tests generally. Students who believe the LSAT is not an accurate reflection of their aptitude to study law should indicate this on their applications.

There is some dispute about whether preparation for the LSAT can improve candidates' scores. A number of prep courses are offered in different parts of the country. The evidence is inconclusive as to how much these courses will help. Although some preparation can be valuable, it may be that a self-imposed preparation schedule using one of several prep books can be as effective as an expensive course. For the student with self-discipline, this study method may even be superior. General information on the LSAT may be found in the *Pre Law Handbook* available from the Educational Testing Service, from any law school admissions office, or most college and public libraries.

In the case of the LSAT, one test determines the score. Grades, on the other hand, represent a complex set of behaviors and performances over a period of years. If a school relies only on grade point average, it would seem to suggest that a student go to the "easiest" school and take the "easiest" major to get the highest GPA. Such a strategy could backfire and leave a person with inadequate training for the rigors of law school, as well as the possibility of an unchallenging and unsatisfying course of study. Moreover, most schools have moved away from strict adherence to a numbers system. In addition to looking at things like extracurricular activities, work experience, career goals, and geographic background, law schools often look at the quality of an undergraduate institution including the extent to which grade inflation has occurred, the difficulty of a student's major field, graduate level study, and other considerations which do not show in an overall GPA.

The aspiring lawyer should view admission to law school as his or her first big case. In a sense the applicant is arguing before a court (the admissions committee) a case (an application to law school). Although some schools permit oral arguments (an interview) most will make their decision on the basis of a brief (the application) filed with the court. The goal of the applicant is to argue persuasively that he or she should be admitted.

PRE-LAW STUDY

There is no such thing as a "pre-law major," even though some universities suggest a specific course of study or special courses for pre-law students. Law schools require graduation from a four-year college or university. Years ago some law schools did not require that students actually graduate from college before entering law school, but today virtually all law schools require a baccalaureate degree. Law students came from virtually every discipline imaginable: political science, business, history, technical science, education, music and the arts, psychology, liberal arts, to name a few. In fact, a central part of the educational process in law school is to bring together people with diverse backgrounds and differing experiences.

Students should select fields of study they enjoy; research

shows that students do better in subjects they like. In addition, since law has applications in almost every human endeavor, one's pre-law background may provide additional qualifications for getting into certain areas of law after graduating. For instance, someone with a degree in accounting may very well be interested in and pursue a career in tax law. Courses which are intellectually challenging will provide good preparation for the intellectual challenge of law school. Courses which broaden a student's horizons provide good preparation for the wide range of problems with which a lawyer must deal. Ideally, a lawyer should know a little about everything, as well as a great deal about the law.

WHICH LAW SCHOOL?

Inevitably applicants ask: "What law school should I attend?" The easiest answer, "The best one you can get into," is perhaps too easy. First of all, no one can agree on the "best" schools. For the record, there are a handful of schools which are generally accepted as most prestigious: Harvard, Yale, Chicago, Michigan, Stanford, Columbia, California-Berkeley, Pennsylvania, Texas, Virginia, and New York University. This status is earned through decades of high quality education. If others prepared a list of "national" law schools they might add one or two others suggesting, as Dean Norman Redlich of New York University Law School quipped recently that, "There are now 30 to 40 schools in the top 10." In addition, there are many strong "regional" and "local" law schools. These terms, *national, regional,* and *local* are euphemisms used by officials who do not want to rate schools. The reluctance to rate schools derives partly from the fact that reputations reflect the past and may or may not give a true indication of the quality of a law school today. It is also difficult to know how to judge a school. These following criteria may help you to evaluate prospective schools.

Faculty. Who are they? What have they written? Do they hold chairs or professorships? What do students say about their teaching? What is the ratio of students to faculty? What are their credentials? How much diversity is there? Are they active participants in the law school community?

Library. How many volumes? What special collections? Is the material accessible? Is a computerized system available? How many legally-trained staff members are there?

Physical plant. Is there enough room to study? Are there sufficient classrooms and seminar rooms? Is there a courtroom? Are there areas for student interaction such as study rooms and lounge areas? Are the surroundings attractive and pleasant enough to endure for three years?

Placement. What services are available through the office? Where do graduates go? A warning: it is often misleading to compare placement patterns of different schools because actual career choices may not reflect potential career choices. Ask if there is a career library, counseling, career information panels, and training in job search skills.

Cost. What are the tuition and fees? What financial aid is available in the form of loans, scholarships and work-study funds?

It cannot be said too often that a legal education is an expensive proposition. The least expensive school will cost several thousand dollars; the most expensive over $20,000. The cost factor is important because after graduating from law school loans accrued during school must be paid back. This puts pressure on many graduates to obtain high paying, salaried jobs, thereby narrowing their career options. For example, it would be difficult for someone with loans to pay back to finance a sole practice, which might take a year or more to break even. Some students work for a time before law school in order to save money to defray a portion of their expenses. If you can find a way to pay for law school without having to work or assume loans, do it. If finances are a problem, but you want to be a lawyer, do not let money stand in your way. Financial aid is available through law schools or their affiliated universities. In any event try to take care of your finances before enrolling because you will have enough to think about without having to worry where your next meal is coming from.

American Bar Association statistics show that about 31.45 percent of all law students are women and 8.15 percent members of ethnic minority groups. Although it is difficult to estimate, there are large numbers of older students in school today who are retired, changing careers, or, in a growing number of instances, homemakers assuming new roles. The American Bar Association has traditionally advocated equal opportunity in access to legal education, and most law schools seek a diverse student body representative of society as a whole. In the next quarter of a century the percentage of women and minorities in the legal profession will probably continue to increase gradually as a result of increased admission of students from these groups to law school.

Overleaf: Top, Supreme Court justices at Hildebrand Moot Court Competition, University of Texas Law School. Photo: Lon Cooper. Bottom, Lobby of Townes Hall, University of Texas Law School. Photo: Larry Murphy.

CHAPTER 11

GOING TO LAW SCHOOL

Dave stood and listened, thoughtfully, almost as if he were taking notes, and only occasionally volunteered agreement or objection. Dave was an analyst but he never practiced law and never intended to. He was a reporter both before he came to law school and after. With his background in law and journalism he became a correspondent covering, among other things, legal issues for a national news magazine.

Assuming that you have completed the application process, retained your sanity and completed your undergraduate education or whatever else you are doing, when lightning strikes—you are admitted to law school. What then? What do you expect? Is it like in the movies? Will you be able to cut it? Is there something you have forgotten? Do you really want to go through with this? These and many other questions will play upon your mind as you prepare for that first day in law school.

Law school is at its best a mind expanding experience; at its worst it is an ordeal. Some students find it the most exciting time of their lives, others the most boring. One thing that everyone will tell the law school applicant is, "It's different from anything you've ever done before." And they will be right. But the same thing is true of first grade, high school, and college.

Who can forget the first time they went to a school where people changed classes every hour? Law school is different, but just like every other new experience in the educational process, it is survivable.

Another story that is sometimes repeated to pre-law students is that the professor on the first day says, "Look to the right of you. Then look to the left of you. One of these people isn't going to be here in the spring." Actually there was a time when just about anyone who wanted to go to law school could get in and those who lacked the intellectual skills never made it past the first year. Today, this is simply not the case. Because of the large number of law school applicants in the United States— in 1979 there were 111,235 who took the Law School Admission Test while there were 40,717 first year law students—most students in most law schools have credentials which indicate that they have the capability to do law school work. Those who do not make it in law school today do not fail because they are not bright enough.

Outside class, extracurricular and employment experiences which provide a broader perspective on life are useful. Perhaps much more than some other professional fields, law demands well-rounded individuals. One possible reason is that lawyers are society's problem solvers, and as such they have to know more than how to draft a complaint or file an answer. They have to be able to work with people.

A legal education is much more than learning the law. It is an experience in understanding how to solve problems. Law school is only partly in the books and the classrooms. The heart of it is in the interaction among students and faculty. The law school population comes from diverse backgrounds and, like a good minestrone soup, the more ingredients the better.

The American Bar Association requires law students to complete at least 84 semester hours or the equivalent. This normally takes three years of full-time or four years part-time attendance.

Full-time students must take at least 10 hours per semester and work no more than 20 hours per week. Law schools offer the same basic first year courses: torts (from the French word for wrong), contracts, and property. There is some variation in other courses offered in the first year although criminal law, constitutional law, civil procedure, and introduction to legal systems are among the courses usually offered. Each school has some program for teaching legal research and writing as well as oral advocacy skills during the first year.

After the first year, the curriculum will vary from school to school. Some schools may offer almost all electives in the last two years. Others may provide a curriculum almost as programmed as the first year. Some schools have certain courses or programs which every student must take. Every school must offer training in legal ethics.

Most schools offer courses in clinical legal education. These courses are designed to provide practical experience to law students by giving them supervised contact with real clients. These programs are frequently conducted under the auspices of local legal aid or public defender offices. Many schools are now offering courses in such areas as trial advocacy, negotiation, client counseling, and appellate advocacy. These courses supplement the traditional curriculum in favor of practical training in lawyering skills. One of the biggest debates in legal education today is how much theory and how much practice should be included in a legal education. Different law schools may emphasize practical training to a greater or lesser degree depending on the educational philosophy of the law school.

Working in legally related positions during law school is another means of obtaining practical training in legal skills before graduation. A high percentage of law students will have at least one such job during their stay in law school, and many will have more. Students work during the academic year in part-time positions or clerkships, and during the summers in full-time positions. The work that they do includes many of the things that a practicing lawyer does in his or her job. There is usually considerable research on legal issues in cooperation with one or more attorneys.

In addition to outside work, law school offers an array of legally related extracurricular activities. There is a student government called the Student Bar Association; there are social organizations; there are special interest groups in such areas as criminal law, international law, and others. Most schools have special organizations for women and ethnic minority law students. Some schools sponsor student research organizations, school newspapers, and even yearbooks. Quite often the law school is insulated from the university with which it is affiliated.

Moot Court Programs

The moot court program gives students, many of whom are interested in litigation, a chance to compete against one another on a variety of problems not unlike debate. Here the problems are legal ones and vary depending on the competition. In traditional moot court, each team produces a brief and argues one side of its case against another team in an elimination tournament. Newer competitions in areas such as client counseling and trial tactics change this format somewhat. There are school, state, and national moot court programs, and the experience can be a valuable one for the future lawyer.

Law Reviews and Law Journals

The law review or law journal is the scholarly arm of he law school. In most fields, journals are edited by scholars in the field. In law, this editorial work is often done by students. For many years most law reviews admitted candidates at the end of their first year on the basis of first year grades. Today many law

ave been convicted of felonies or crimes involving moral
ude may have difficulty being certified to take the exam.
ere are bar review courses available in most states. These
s are designed to acquaint those taking the bar with what
ect. They are not required, but most graduates have invested
or four years in law school and tend to play the percentages
ke the course.

examinations have been criticized in recent years. The
tion has been made that use of the bar exam is supported
acticing lawyers to reduce competition and discourage
ty. From time to time, proposals for the creation of a
al bar exam arise, but the Multistate is as close as anyone
me to succeeding. Like the LSAT, bar exams have also
riticized for discriminating against minority groups. Almost
es require persons taking the bar to have graduated from a
hool approved by the American Bar Association. Periodi-
graduates of unapproved law schools apply to take the bar
grounds that this requirement is unfair. These applications
or the most part been unsuccessful. This fact alone should
nost pre-law students from enrolling in non-ABA approved
ools. In addition, a school's quality of education is gener-
nsidered by legal educators to be open to question until or
he school gains **ABA** approval.

a pre-law student, you are involved in the career choice
through which you will make some major decisions
our life. Understanding this process will help you through-
ir career to cope with change and to grow. However, it
rtant to remember that there are two distinct processes
l here.

first process is the *career choice process* in which you
ethods of self-analysis, evaluation of the environment,
king priorities. The second process is the *job search*,
ncludes techniques such as interviewing, resume writing,
arch for potential job openings.

reviews also admit candidates through a voluntary internship
as well. The opportunity to gain experience in research and writing and the desire of many legal employers to hire graduates who
have been law review editors are enough inducement to persuade
candidates to put in long hours in addition to their coursework
to gain acceptance on the editorial board.

Graduation

Graduation from law school usually comes none too soon.
After three years of rigorous schooling in law after 16 or more
years in other educational settings, students are ready to go out
and face the real world. Law schools have certain minimum
standards for graduation including honors, course requirements
and grades. In the past grades may have been a problem for many
students. Today with admissions standards as formidable as they
are, few people who cannot do the work are admitted. As indi-
cated previously, those who do not make it fail for reasons other
than ability. Many in fact find out that they just do not like
law study and practice.

It is difficult to describe law school to one who has never
been there. It is a complex and challenging experience, but one
which inevitably changes those who go through it by transform-
ing their habits and the ways they think. There are several good
books on the law school experience mentioned in the bibliography. Reading these or visiting law school classes will help
you to understand more of what to expect. The only way, however, that you will really know what law school is like is to go
there yourself.

Overleaf: Above, University of Wyoming College of Law, Laramie,
Wyoming. Below, Baylor Law School practice court session.

wh
tur

cou
to e
thre
and

sugg
by
mob
nati
has
beer
all s
law
cally
on t
have
dete
law
ally
unles

As
proce
about
out y
is im
involv

Th
learn
and r
which
and re

CHAPTER

AFTER GRAD
FROM LAW S

Gary went to work for the
in the general counsel's office.
ances against other lawyers, incl
a couple of our classmates
their ethics well enough in law s

THE BAR EX

The first hurdle after graduation
there are careers which do not require
to pass the bar in order to practice
not even plan to practice law take
behind them.

The requirements and examinatio
as do pass rates. In 1978, the pass
percent to a high of 100 percent
various states. Most states include a
state Bar Exam, a multiple choice
essay questions based on state law.
requirements, strict application pro
nations. While attempts to preven
exams on the basis of lifestyle ha

The first must precede the second. In other words, a person must know what is looked for before starting to search for it. The goal is for law school graduates to find positions both personally and professionally rewarding. From the time a student first decides to attend law school until he or she finally chooses a job, the person is evaluating, either consciously or unconsciously, all of the opportunities. That there are so many opportunities is fortunate, yet it is unfortunate that many people either do not investigate or are not aware of the full range of possibilities.

The first of the two processes just mentioned is the *career choice process*. We prefer to talk about career planning in terms of a specific model—the career choice process, because we feel that *planning* may infer that there is some magic formula which will allow a person to map out his or her future with any degree of certainty. For most of us, this is simply not possible. Too much of our fate lies beyond our control. Factors such as economic conditions, luck and personal handicaps will affect our goals. Career choice, on the other hand, is a decision-making process which attempts to allow the individual to make the best possible choices at the time when the decision must be made, and to increase the alternatives available in making the decision.

We suggest that you approach the career choice process in a rational way, and that you take certain steps in sequence. This is not to say that this is the only way to make career decisions, but it is one way that has worked for many people. If you are not sure about which direction your professional life should take, you really need to organize your thoughts. It is undoubtedly better to go through the trauma of uncertainty while you are in school than to go to work in a position you find out you don't like—where you have not foreseen what was foreseeable.

Self-evaluation. If you are to make the wisest choices for yourself about the direction your life will be taking, it is mandatory that you have enough self-awareness and self-knowledge to be able to make a decision that will be well suited to your personal goals and individual abilities. Only by beginning with a perfectly honest appraisal of yourself can this be a valid evaluation, and this might well be the most difficult step in the career choice process, as well as one of the most intrinsic to its success. Seeing yourself as you really are, and not as you were, or could be, or should be, or will be, is not an easy process. If you don't like the image that you see, by all means take steps to remedy the situation. However, do not rest your later decisions on projected self-images which are not the real you.

In order to evaluate and understand yourself, you should consider a number of variables—among them are your *abilities, skills, interests, needs, values, and goals.*

Analyzing the market. This analysis no less than self-evaluation requires honesty. Here, however, you are required to look outward, to view your environment, to see things the way they are. Many people are not able to determine the relative importance of the factors involved. However, some that might be important to the person seeking employment would certainly be, *academic preparation, work experience, and available job alternatives.* It may be difficult to evaluate what jobs will be available in law by the time you graduate from law school several years hence, but if you are constantly evaluating alternatives, your choices will be easier when the time comes.

Ranking priorities. This process involves skills generally classified as decision-making. You will be unusual if your self-evaualation and objective analysis do not leave you with numerous questions, ambiguities, and uncertainties. Decision-making is the process whereby you choose or select a course of action among several possibilities. Hopefully, your self-evaluation and objective analysis will have made the definition of the decision to be made somewhat simpler.

When you are ranking priorities, you are creating a list of career alternatives, a list that you will use in the job search. Such a list not only prevents you from putting all your eggs in one basket, but also eliminates confusion by focusing your career search on certain opportunities. In other words, throughout this evaluation, you are asking yourself whether or not you want to go to law school. At the same time you must consider, if you do want to go to law school and you are not accepted, what should be your alternative plan? Remember, too, that the process does not end when you get into law school.

The job search is the crucial part of the whole process, because it is here that you are actually looking for a job. There are two aspects to the job search—building job search skills and carrying out a plan. There will be time for this part of the process once you get into law school. The main point here is to begin your career planning now and not to assume it is finished when you get into law school.

Few people will be able to go from start to finish without learning more information, developing more skills, or realizing that new skills will be needed for a desired career. This reevaluation may take the student back to the beginning or it may require only a re-examination at the present level. However, the re-evaluation process is essential to making a satisfying decision. The most critical re-evaluation is one which deserves to be mentioned. What happens when the student goes through the complete career search process with no results? It is hoped that by careful analysis, you can avoid this situation. However, in the event that this happens, it is probably best to go back to the beginning and start anew, looking at other alternatives.

It should be added that this is a process which never ends. The average lawyer will make several job changes in the course of his or her career. If you can develop good skills of career planning early, you will avoid much frustration later on. You can expect, however, to make mistakes in the beginning, to learn from them, and to become more skilled with practice.

As mentioned above, it is difficult to predict what the job market will be like in the future—three, five, or even ten years down the road. Any projection of the market would be more subject to change than a weather forecast. Since so many pre-law students want to know what their prospects will be, it may be worthwhile to offer a few observations.

PREDICTIONS OF EMPLOYMENT PROSPECTS

Every year there appear more than a few articles describing the employment prospects for new lawyers as dismal at best. The titles are always a somber "New Lawyers Flood the Market," or something equally frightening. The articles seem to suggest that law students who didn't graduate in the top 10 percent at one of the top ten schools had better plan to make their livelihoods in some other field.

These articles are often simplistic in their analysis and may miss both the nature and extent of the problem. They strike terror into the hearts of law students and pre-law students as well. There is no way to determine how many good prospects have been deterred from even applying to law school because of such stories.

The "placement scare" stories almost always juxtapose employment predictions by the U.S. Department of Labor, Bureau of Labor Statistics and the actual number of law graduates, suggesting an acute overabundance of new lawyers. In 1973, the BLS projected 16,500 jobs for 31,000 graduates, figures which are still quoted today, despite a 1980 estimate of 37,000 jobs for 35,000 graduates. The BLS attempts to predict growth in the profession on the basis of: 1) national economic trends, 2) reports of various state and federal employment and research agencies, and 3) replacement for those who leave the profession due to death or retirement, or to enter another profession.

The Bureau of Labor Statistics states that its "projections tend to be conservatively biased." Thus, for growing professions the outlook may be better than projected. A more serious problem for BLS is how it defines "the legal profession."

When BLS uses the total number of annual law graduates in making projections, it fails to consider those who do not intend to enter the legal job market, or who fail the bar exam and cannot enter it. The National Association for Law Placement in its employment survey of the Class of 1976 found 6 percent of the graduates—whose whereabouts was known—to be in this category. In addition, many of the 20 percent who graduated from part-time programs returned to jobs they held prior to law school, and thus did not enter the job market. There are many things which lawyers can and do choose to do outside of the practice of law. In fact, as society becomes more complex, there are increasingly fewer endeavors for which knowledge of law or a law degree do not provide tangible benefits.

In terms of the demand for legal services, there *must* be more to be considered than employment projections.

If there are law school graduates who are unemployed or underemployed, it is not because there are not opportunities. It is not because there are no societal needs for more legal services for presently under-represented groups. The problem is rather, one of distribution. There are too many applicants in some areas already saturated with attorneys, and too few in other areas where there are unmet demands.

The NALP Employment Survey gives a clear picture of the demand for legal services as reflected in the jobs accepted by the nation's law graduates. The 1979 survey mentioned in Chapter 2 covering 139 law schools with almost 25,000 graduates, reports the employment status of 22,771. Of these, 21,633 or 95 percent of those qualified and seeking employment, are, in fact, employed in law-related positions six to eight months after graduation. These percentages and the percentages for the various types of jobs are almost identical to those in the 1975 NALP survey suggesting some stability in the legal job market. There are several findings that do not appear at first glance. 1) Different schools may differ considerably as to the employment picture for their graduates depending upon the employers they serve. For example,

Georgetown Law School in Washington, D.C., has a higher percentage of graduates go to work for the federal government than most schools. 2) The sample of responding schools does not differ substantially from the non-responding schools. 3) Minority graduates did as well overall (with 94 percent in 1979 employed) as did all graduates. Only a small percentage (27 percent) entered private practice, however. 4) Women scored slightly lower than the overall group (with 91 percent employed and 41 percent in private practice). 5) Of the 6 percent of all known graduates who did not enter the job market, there was a higher percent of ethnic minorities who failed the bar, and a higher percent of women who were not seeking employment, than for graduates overall.

Geographically, 34.8 percent located in the Northeast, 16.3 percent in the Southeast, 23.1 percent in the Great Lakes and Plains states, and 24.9 percent in the West and Southwest. These figures, too, are very similar to those for 1975. Over 43 percent settled in only 20 cities. In addition, a 1975 NALP survey determined that 83 percent of the Northeastern graduates stayed in the Northeast, 74.5 percent from the Southeast stayed in their region, 81 percent from the Great Lakes and Plains, 89 percent from the West and Southwest. This most likely remains true today.

NALP has asked placement directors to list the reasons why their unemployed students had not found jobs. The most frequent response was strict geographic requirements (very often the city in which their law school was located). Next most frequent was a late start in the job search and, finally, personality or qualification problems (in other words, not being able to get hired for jobs to which they were applying).

How serious a problem is the 6 percent unemployment reported by NALP? In another survey by the California Young Lawyers Association unemployment at similar levels for all California lawyers out of school ten years or less prompted former CYLA President Tolly Besson to raise an interesting question:

> Whether the survey findings are viewed . . . as discouraging or encouraging depends upon the person's preconceptions. Some will consider 4.1 percent unemployment very discouraging in the light of the employment experience of other professionals such as doctors or dentists. Others will view the figures as not as bad as might be expected especially in light of the levels of unemployment in the population at large, and the normal problems of establishing a law practice.

It should be obvious that the job search is tough. It's hard work and it's not always good for the ego. There is limited access to positions which are most prestigious and remunerative. Last year, 6.5 percent of the graduates went to work in law firms which employed more than 50 lawyers. Only 3.5 percent accepted prestigious federal judicial clerkships. In fact, the 52.4 percent in private practice is just more than half the class. Thus, although the market for new law school graduates is not as bleak as recent articles have suggested, it is clear that many students will have to search actively for positions and consider a variety of opportunities and locations.

In other words, each individual must assess his or her marketability in light of the demand for someone with the skills and background possessed, as well as assess overall trends in the employment picture. Many factors influence these trends and affect to some degree the demand for legal services. Several factors will tend to increase demand:

- The growth of prepaid legal services, and other plans to bring legal services to middle-income groups.
- The continued existence and further extension of government regulation at all levels.
- The increase in the public's willingness to litigate as awareness of individual and collective rights become more widely understood.

- The increase in the population itself including the immigration into this country of large numbers of Spanish-speaking individuals.
- The expansion of the business community as further industrialization of our society occurs.
- The development of new areas of law practice—public interest and consumer law, legal services to underprivileged persons heretofore without access to programs, teaching and administrative work in areas outside law schools, and judicially mandated criminal defense work.

While some of these areas are not growing as rapidly as some predicted and many hoped, there has been and will continue to be an increase in the demand for services and more than enough interested students to fill new jobs.

On the other hand, several factors are working to contract the opportunities in the legal profession. The development of paraprofessionals and the increased use of office machines and management procedures cut into the work previously done by associates. With rising salaries for law graduates many employers seriously consider alternatives to the employment of recent law graduates. Another development which is cutting into the legal job market may be termed the crisis in confidence. Whether it was Watergate, years of laxity by the bar in upholding ethical standards, or other reasons, the public's opinion of lawyers has reached an all-time low. No-fault laws at least in part reflect this lack of confidence. Banks, title companies, savings and loan associations, and accounting firms are all promising to do work presently or in the recent past done by lawyers both cheaper and better. Less work means fewer jobs, and this trend raises important issues as to what the role of the lawyer should be. The ability of the legal profession to deliver its services is extremely important to the continued growth of the profession.

There are also shifts in demand, some of rather short duration, some of long range. Population movement is always taking place, and lawyers will follow the people. Many factors such as the relative wealth of the population, or the existence of business and government entities in the community provide barometers of demand for legal service and provide clues as to the need for additional attorneys.

The business cycle can affect demand; the economy has its ups and downs, and since legal work is often tied to business activity, the legal profession rises and falls with the economy, not only nationally but locally as well.

Shifts in the demand for legal services may occur in some substantive areas of law. A major new piece of legislation to pass Congress may result in many new jobs for lawyers. The energy crisis has fueled the oil and gas practice. A recession may wipe out lawyers who have real estate practices while the bankruptcy lawyers stay busy. Tomorrow? Who knows? If law school administrators knew what areas would be in demand in four years they could plan the curriculum accordingly. A few predictions may help:

- Many rural areas of our country will experience a severe shortage of attorneys as the urbanization of America continues to expand.
- Significantly more lawyers will be hired by business and industry to positions traditionally held by non-lawyers. Some of these positions will eventually require a law degree as a prerequisite to being hired.
- The face of private practice will undergo unprecedented changes with the establishment of large legal clinics and multi-office corporate mega-firms, resulting in more jobs.
- The sunbelt growth will mean a much slower rate of growth and in many cases a decline in employment opportunities in the Northeast and Midwest. For the next quarter of a century we will witness the blossoming of cities from Jacksonville to San Diego, and an increasingly larger percentage of jobs will be found in sunbelt cities.

This discussion of the job market implies that there is not a single job market in the legal profession, but many. There are job markets for different types of law and different kinds of employers. There are frequently different job markets in different regions and cities. The fact that there is no national bar exam tends to accentuate the regional hiring patterns of employers. On the other hand, many areas of the practice of law do not vary substantially from region to region.

What this means is that geographic choices of where to live after graduation and perhaps where to attend law school can be important. If there is any area of practice you are interested in, you may have to make geographical choices with that in mind. Many people are not as concerned with what they practice as where they live. Some law graduates accept jobs they would not otherwise choose because they want to live in a certain city. There are a number of cities which are very popular places to live which are also inundated with lawyers. Sometimes, some hard choices need to be made. An individual with some geographic flexibility will find the task of securing employment much easier than one who doggedly tries to stay in an overcrowded market.

FINANCIAL REWARDS

One of the reasons people choose to go to law school is for the financial rewards. An old lawyer once told the author, who was in law school at the time, "Son, if you want to get rich, get out of this business. Lawyers may work for rich people, but you don't get rich practicing law." There are wealthy lawyers, but many of them have gained their fortunes through business enterprises outside the practice of law. Outside of a handful of lawyers with unusual practices, most lawyers can expect to have a comfortable living, but not fantastic riches.

Beginning Salaries

It may come as no surprise that starting legal salaries have risen along with the cost of everything else. It takes more money to live these days, and recent law graduates feel this as acutely as anyone, especially if they have educational loans to repay.

For potential employers, the question of how much to pay is difficult. Placement directors frequently hear phrases like *the going rate, competitive,* or *comparable to similar firms in our location.* The truth is that starting salaries vary considerably from as low as $8,000 to as high as $37,000 nationally. The median 1980 salary for all recent law graduates is around $19,000.

Because of the wide range in legal salaries, it may be difficult for an individual to know what to expect. There are a number of factors to consider. The scale is generally highest in the big cities; in fact, the larger the city, the higher salaries tend to be. Higher salaries are typically given to new lawyers by larger organizations, although small organizations may be required to pay competitively if they expect to compete with larger employers. The competition for students at the top of their classes may have attenuated the salary range over the years.

Mature Incomes

Salaries for experienced attorneys are even more difficult to pinpoint than starting salaries. There are lawyers who have practiced 20 years who barely earn enough to stay alive; there are others whose incomes run into seven figures. The American Bar Association recently reported that the median salary for all lawyers had dropped to $28,000 in 1978 from $31,000 two years earlier. This drop undoubtedly reflects the fact that approximately half of the lawyers in the United States have been licensed for ten years or less, and these are the lawyers who earn the least income.

Student Incomes

Salaries for law students who are still in school can be determined to some extent by comparison with other employers, but also by using an easy formula based on an associate's probable starting salary. Generally, summer and part-time law clerks can expect to make two-thirds to three-fourths what an employer would pay a newly licensed attorney to go to work. The actual ranges of these salaries is more like one-half to nine-tenths, but the two-thirds to three-fourths figure is a good rule of thumb, using two-thirds for first-year students, and three-fourths for second-year students. Clerk salaries may be described in terms of hourly, weekly, or monthly rates, and may range from a fairly good income to as low as minimum wage.

For the future, a $40,000 annual starting salary is not just around the corner. On the other hand, employers must continue to grow to meet the needs of their clients; and many will be willing to compete fiercely to attract the best possible legal talent. Inflation will continue to affect salaries as well, so employers can expect average starting salaries to continue to rise.

How Important Is Money?

Another way of looking at the financial picture is to compare two individuals, one who worked in a factory from the time he or she graduated from high school, and the other who went to college and law school, and then went to work in the highest paying law firm around. If the plant worker earned one-half of what the lawyer earned, the plant worker would have made over $100,000 before the lawyer ever passed the bar. It would not be until the fifteenth year after high school that the lawyer's income would pass the plant worker's. In time, the lawyer might come out ahead financially, but some students may not want to delay gratification that long. Furthermore, since most new law graduates do not command the top salaries, it would take some lawyers much longer to catch up, and others never would. In summary, money alone is not a reason to choose a legal career. While monetary rewards will be adequate, those who expect highly lucrative opportunities may well be disappointed.

Overleaf: Portraits of famous lawyers watch over a student's endeavors at Tarlton Law Library, University of Texas. Photo: Larry Murphy.

CHAPTER 13

BEYOND LAW SCHOOL

Tim, the rugged individualist. Unlike the other practicing attorneys at the party, no one paid Tim's salary. After working for a government agency and a corporation, he decided to be his own boss and follow the time-honored professional tradition of 'hanging out his shingle.' It has been tough going thus far for Tim, but he is beginning to see the fruits of his labor and appreciates his independence.

Like society at large, the legal profession is undergoing rapid changes. It seems that the only constant in our world is change itself. The way law will be practiced in the decade of the eighties and beyond will be determined by client needs which in turn will be influenced by broad economic and societal developments.

A CHANGING PICTURE

Are you ready to handle the problems of space law, genetic engineering, and global eco-crises? Can you imagine working for a firm that employs 5,000 attorneys? How will litigation tactics change when trials are presented to the judge and/or jury on pre-edited videotape? When "the law" is no longer to be found in books, but in computer memory banks? When technical and scientific issues are handled in special technical courts? When specialist licenses are issued by the Department of Justice?

No, these projections are not lifted from a Buck Rogers script, but were seriously presented by a Chicago attorney as possible developments in the legal profession by the year 2078. Obviously, the profession will have time to adjust. In the meantime, there are many new developments which may be no less dramatic in their impact on the profession in the next twenty years. No matter how you envision your future, your career will undoubtedly involve areas and methods not even imagined fifty years ago.

Who will be your clients? The development of neighborhood clinics, group legal services, law stores, and insurance plans, will bring substantial demands from middle income clients for a variety of services. Increased appropriations for the federally funded legal services have provided greater access for individuals in low income groups to legal assistance in civil and, increasingly, criminal cases. Changes will occur in the areas of advertising, specialization, self-regulation of the legal profession, and questions of competency and responsibilities for giving advice. The adversary system is not immune from evolution: new methods of dispute resolution are being tried. Old concepts of how trials should be held are being challenged. Arbitration agreements and no-fault laws lead many to believe that the function of the courts will change dramatically in the coming years. Moreover, the proposed *Model Rules of Professional Conduct* encourage the lawyer to act as counselor and negotiator as well as an advocate. Within the legal profession, the growth of very large law firms with several branches, assemblyline procedures and other office management improvements, the use of paralegals to help reserve the lawyer's time for more complicated legal work are already here. The expansion of legal departments of corporations and the employment of more lawyers in government agencies are affecting the traditional attorney-client relationships. These organizational changes are touching every important activity of the individual practitioner and the environment in which he or she works.

Why are changes occurring? Many, of course, are brought about by forces within the profession; but in some cases lawyers have waited and are now reacting to external pressures.

Because the profession has changed and will continue to change at such a rapid rate, it is important for students to reflect critically and examine the new directions their profession is taking as well as their potential roles within it if they expect to act as agents of change rather than simply to react to change as it occurs.

In addition to participating in the process of change, pre-law students and practicing attorneys should be aware that their own careers will be affected by societal changes. Shifts in the way law is practiced will mean occupational displacement. Some fields which were once lucrative will no longer be so. Mechanization of services and larger organizations may mean that some traditional legal work will be more routine and less challenging than in the past. On the other hand, new areas of practice are already evolving which will provide challenges that are unknown today. What does this mean to the career patterns of lawyers?

JOB SATISFACTION

There is a myth in the legal profession that lawyers keep one job throughout their legal careers. If this was ever true, it certainly is not today. The average lawyer will hold five to eight jobs in the forty years between law school graduation and retirement, and a high percentage of attorneys will make at least one major career change in their lives.

Evidence of rampant job dissatisfaction in America is easy to find. Studs Terkel, a lawyer himself, suggested in his book,

Working, that job dissatisfaction is pervasive in our society. He found that, though people seemed happy in their *work*, they were not necessarily so happy in their present *positions*; they were often on the road to somewhere, and passing time in their present circumstances.

It is clear that lawyers are not alone in this state of mind. However, it would be unwise to assume that dissatisfaction in the legal profession is completely due to our changing times, or sunspot activity, or some other global cause.

In many ways the legal profession is unique. The dissatisfaction of lawyers with their professional lives can be explained, if not totally understood. However, dissatisfaction is the stuff that progress is made of, that careers grow on, that futures are built with. Find a man or woman who is completely happy in a job and you will find someone who has no dreams. Each of us is in one sense always in the job market. There are very few who would not leave what they are doing if some golden opportunity were to develop.

John L. Holland, one of America's foremost career theorists, explains that high levels of job dissatisfaction, or dissonance, as he calls it, will produce one of three responses: to change ourselves, to change our environment, or to leave the environment. When we change ourselves, we accept whatever it was that was bothering us. When we change the environment, we eliminate the offending problem. If neither adjustment is possible, we look for something new. For instance, if a lawyer is told he or she will not be made a partner in the law firm but can stay as an associate, the lawyer will either accept the decision, attempt to prove that he or she should be made partner, or pull out an old resume and start to revise it.

Decisions about careers are almost always complex ones involving many considerations. Factors such as the employability of the individual in the market place, tolerance for the bad situation, willingness to assume a risk, and the need for security inevitably weigh heavily in the equation. Each year, thousands of lawyers change jobs. In many instances, the transition is smooth, but very often the change is difficult and painful. Sometimes it is destructive.

What are the roots of lawyer dissatisfaction? The most commonly named reason given by dissatisfied lawyers is that their present employment did not utilize the skills they believed they possessed as lawyers. It is important to note that most of these people held legal jobs that would appear to be attractive on paper. A second cause of dissatisfaction is low salary and/or a perception that the position had "no future." A third complaint is unpleasant working conditions, including conflicts with supervising attorneys.

These indices of dissatisfaction differ from those reported in a recent survey by the California Young Lawyers Association. The CYLA study uses the term "underemployed," which it applies to the lawyer who 1) is practicing law and does not have enough legal work to stay busy full-time, or 2) is employed in a non-legal position, having been unable to obtain a legal one.

The term "underemployment" is too subjective to be useful in discussing the broad range of job dissatisfaction. How many lawyers would call themselves underemployed whose jobs would be considered ideal by others? How many who would call themselves underemployed could charitably be described as overemployed by an unbiased outsider? How many in jobs with "low status" are perfectly happy? How many could have a better job if they would be willing to move to another city? How many of those without legal work do not operate an efficient law office, or never learned to attact and keep clients?

These questions are not intended to criticize the California study, but rather to focus attention on specific job-related factors that have a major bearing on whether one will be happy in his or her job or seek a new one. Focusing on the three reasons articulated above, it is possible to get a clearer picture of situations where a lawyer would be willing to make a job change whether that person is in a legal or non-legal job.

The first complaint of not using the skills one possesses or learns in law school is most critical. Holland, in *Making Vocational Choices*, articulates the theory that individuals tend to like what they succeed at, and that they will succeed in the future in activities utilizing the same skills and activities they have succeeded at in the past. In other words, career development ought to involve careful evaluation of past personal and job behavior to determine competencies which will be most likely to produce success in a new situation.

Lack of job future and salary are often related and have been grouped together for purposes of this discussion. Having a feeling that a job contributes to a positive direction in one's career is essential to one's self-concept and job satisfaction. Jobs that are perceived as "dead-ends," or "unchallenging," usually become former jobs of employees who can neither change or accept them. Salary can influence a person's perception of a job future, and in these times of rapid inflation, a low-paying but rewarding job is more likely to be perceived as lacking a future.

The final area described as a factor in lawyers' decisions to leave their jobs is working conditions. Everything else may be fine, but if you hate your co-workers, or your clients, or your surroundings, you have to go.

The legal profession on the whole sometimes tends to abandon humanistic values in treating lawyer employees and, as a result, a concern for the individual's job satisfaction and career development may be neglected. Whatever the reasons for job dissatisfaction, it is undeniable that it is common. It is frustrating to the lawyer who experiences it, particularly if he or she does not know where to turn. This need not be so.

The lawyer can always leave a situation that is unattractive and move into something different. For many people, it is not until several years after law school that the best career path for them begins to become apparent. The pre-law student should understand that although a knowledge of legal careers may be useful, it may not be possible to choose an area of practice with certainty.

BUILDING A CAREER PATH

After you leave law school, the work that you do gives you expertise. The tendency in the profession today is to build upon that expertise or specialize. Whether you plan to or not, you will find that the cases you have handled in the past will dictate what you will be able to handle in the future. This functional specialization often parallels formal specialization offered in many states. While requirements vary from state to state, there is a trend toward lawyers practicing in much narrower areas than in the past. It may be that, in time, a general practice specialty may evolve similar to the family practice in medicine. The idea that the average person can have someone to call "my lawyer" is not going to die easily.

One of the biggest challenges to the general practitioner is competence. With the law getting more and more complex and clients more and more willing to sue for malpractice, there is great pressure to limit your practice to specific areas of expertise. In addition, the law is always changing, so what you learned in law school ten years earlier may not be enough to keep up with the law.

Continuing Legal Education

Continuing legal education is a multimillion dollar business in which law schools, bar associations and private groups are all involved. Programs are always being offered to help practitioners stay abreast of their practices.

Still, questions are raised about the competence of lawyers at all levels, from as high as the President of the United States and the Chief Justice of the Supreme Court. There are proposals to require periodic relicensing of lawyers and to restrict the practice in many courts without regular readmission to the bar.

A Cutting Edge

It may be somewhat distressing to close on a note of uncertainty, but the fact is that the legal profession is changing and that it is very hard to say what it will be like in ten, twenty, or fifty years, when today's high school students will be getting ready to retire. This chapter has alluded to some of the factors which will shape the profession of the future. If the prospect of entering a field in such a state of flux is unappealing, then consider other occupations. If, however, the prospect of being involved in such a process is attractive to you, law will be an exciting place to be. As society changes, law and lawyers will be on the cutting edge. While some critics of the legal profession charge that lawyers spend their professional lives looking backward to precedent and are thus incapable of coping with the future, the obvious reply is that lawyers possess analytic skills that will be crucial if our society is to cope with the future and that their reliance on precedent is a tool for predicting the future. In a world of change, the career opportunities are vast, and there is probably no career field in our society where there is as much access to these opportunities. Even though traditional jobs for lawyers may be limited, the great flexibility of this degree means that one who is legally trained will probably always have work.

Overleaf: Above, Harvard Law School. Photo: Michael Nagy. Below, members of the Law Student Division of the American Bar Association participate in a luncheon at the Capitol Building in Washington, D.C.

lawyers ought not to be deterred simply because the way is difficult. By the same token, those who are not sure they want to become lawyers ought not to embark on this course simply to find themselves. It is hoped that this book has provided information and insights to those considering law careers so they can make informed decisions about their futures.

CONCLUSION

It has been the American experience to test the limits of democracy. Over the past two hundred years it has been a recognized precept that a citizen deserves the freedom to choose what to do with his or her life. One was to have hardly more limits than self-inherent barriers. This was a land where anyone could become President. To be sure, this promise has never been without blemish: poverty, discrimination, and politics have all deprived some of the opportunities that others got. Yet the Horatio Alger story has been repeated innumerable times in the history of this nation.

DEVELOPING PROFESSIONALS

The professionals—doctors, lawyers, teachers, writers—have always been the intellectual leaders of American society. For more than a few impoverished children, the means to success in the old Algerian sense was through professional education and status. It is, therefore, important that professions be able to attract competent individuals and when trained distribute them throughout the population. Ambition must join opportunity for freedom to be fully a reality.

There is a second societal objective in recruiting and placing professionals, and that is efficiency. Efficiency may sometimes work against the democratic objective, however, because collectively the society seeks not only those who want to be professionals, but those who are most qualified. This has been particularly true in the legal profession where the number of persons aspiring to become attorneys has often exceeded the capacity of law schools to educate them. Acceptance to law school is based not so much on desire as on predicted success, which is in turn based on past achievement.

During the 1970s, interest in law reached an all-time high. There were various reasons for this. Many students sought a legal education because they saw it as an avenue to professional status and financial security. Others came to law with the goal of using their training to make constructive social change. Urged by their elders to work within the system, the part they chose was law. Still others perceived law as an exciting, dynamic profession as legal actions became a routine feature of mass media fare. For these and many other reasons, thousands of students entered the nation's law schools and later the legal profession. This influx of new lawyers has produced some stress on the system's ability to assimilate them and has resulted in keen competition for jobs. Yet the possible alternatives for developing new lawyers are not that attractive.

The Family Business

One method, historically, has been the use of familial ties to determine occupation. Traditionally under this system, if your parent was a baker, you became a baker, and so forth. The obvious advantage here was that you need not face any disconcerting problem of what to do with your life. Everything was taken care of early, and you assumed direction of the family's traditional work at the appropriate time. The disadvantage, of course, was that if you happened not to concur with the predetermined

order of things, there was very little you could do about it. Also, society had no assurance that the offspring of any given worker would be the most competent person to carry on the work. A third problem was that if the parents had seven children, there was still only one farm, one business, or one law library. The system therefore established an order, from eldest to youngest, in which the children should be allowed to profit.

Apprenticeship

Another system of training professionals was the use of apprentices. This system was common in the legal profession in the nineteenth century in this country. The master would teach a trade or profession to the pupil, who would supply labor in return for education. After a period, the apprentice could strike out independently. Complex modern society has practically ended the apprentice system in many professions. Professional schools provide a uniformity in the quality of education, probably unattainable under the former system.

It should be noted that family ties still account for a great deal in the business and professional world, and many an individual has followed in a successful parent's footsteps. Apprenticeships, although more apparent in such occupations as skilled crafts, live on. In law, they primarily take the form of internships where a student spends a certain amount of time while in school working in some area related to his or her education.

It may be that the road to a legal career is a long one, and that there are many pitfalls along the way. It is nevertheless true that, despite its flaws, the American system of legal education has effectively trained generations of skilled lawyers and will continue to do so. It is also probably true that there are today more opportunities for persons who want to be lawyers than at any other time in this nation's history. Those who want to become

APPENDIX A

LAW SCHOOLS

By 1980, there were 170 law schools approved by the American Bar Association (ABA), the accrediting body for legal education. Each school, in order to be approved, must meet certain rigorous tests in such areas as faculty size and quality, physical plant, library holdings, and student academic standards. Many of these accredited schools have also become members of the Association of American Law Schools (AALS) whose standards for membership are even more stringent than those required for American Bar Association accreditation.

This list does not include schools that are not approved by the ABA. In a few states, graduates of these non-ABA approved schools are permitted to take the bar examination in the state where the school is located. Because the quality of education offered at most of these schools is inferior to that provided by approved schools, and because the bar passage rate is frequently very low, it is the author's strong recommendation that students not consider attending one of these institutions. Therefore, the schools are not listed in order to avoid the possible suggestion that this book endorses any such school.

Each school is listed by name and address. For more detailed information, inquiries regarding admission procedure and requirements, costs and financial aid and other general information about the school, students should contact the admissions office at the given address. Most schools will provide detailed descriptive material on request.

LAW SCHOOL NAMES AND ADDRESSES

ALABAMA

Samford University
Cumberland School of Law
800 Lakeshore Drive
Birmingham, AL 35229
205/870-2701

University of Alabama
School of Law
P. O. Box 1435
University, AL 35486
205/348-5117

ARIZONA

Arizona State University
College of Law
Tempe, AZ 85281
602/965-6181

University of Arizona
College of Law
Tucson, AZ 85721
602/626-1373

ARKANSAS

University of Arkansas
School of Law
Waterman Hall
Fayetteville, AR 72701
501/575-560

University of Arkansas
School of Law
400 West Markham
Little Rock, AR 72201
501/371-1071

CALIFORNIA

California Western
School of Law
350 Cedar Street
San Diego, CA 92101
714/239-0391

Golden Gate University
School of Law
536 Mission Street
San Francisco, CA 94105
415/442-7000

Loyola Law School
1440 West 9th Street
Los Angeles, CA 90015
213/642-2900

Pepperdine University
School of Law
24255 Pacific Coast Hwy.
Malibu, CA 90265
213/456-4611

Southwestern University
School of Law
675 South Westmoreland Ave.
Los Angeles, CA 90005
213/380-4800

Stanford Law School
Stanford, CA 94305
415/497-2465

University of California
School of Law
Boalt Hall
Berkeley, CA 94720
415/642-1741

University of California
School of Law
King Hall
Davis, CA 95616

University of California
Hastings College of Law
198 McAllister Street
San Francisco, CA 94102
415/557-1320

University of California
School of Law
405 Hilgard Avenue
Los Angeles, CA 90024
213/825-4841

University of the Pacific
McGeorge School of Law
3200 Fifth Avenue
Sacramento, CA 95817
916/739-7121

University of San Diego
School of Law
Alcala Park
San Diego, CA 92110
714/291-6480

University of San Francisco
School of Law
2199 Fulton Street
Kendrick Hall
San Francisco, CA 94117
415/666-6307

University of Santa Clara
School of Law
Santa Clara, CA 95053
408/984-4361

University of Southern California
Law Center
University Park
Los Angeles, CA 90007
213/741-6473

Whittier College
School of Law
5353 West Third Street
Los Angeles, CA 90020
213/938-3621

COLORADO

University of Colorado
School of Law
Campus Box 401
Boulder, CO 80309
303/492-8047

University of Denver
College of Law
200 West 14th Avenue
Denver, CO 80204
303/753-2645

CONNECTICUT

University of Bridgeport
School of Law
600 University Ave.
Bridgeport, CT 06602
203/576-4045

University of Connecticut
School of Law
Greater Hartford Campus
West Hartford, CT 06117
203/523-4841

Yale Law School
Box 401A Yale Station
New Haven, CT 06520
203/436-1507

DELAWARE

Delaware Law School
Widener University
P. O. Box 7474
Concord Pike
Wilmington, DE 19803
302/478-5280

DISTRICT OF COLUMBIA

American University
Washington College of Law
Massachusetts & Nebraska Avenues,
   N.W.
Washington, DC 20016
202/686-2605

Antioch School of Law
1624 Crescent Place, N.W.
Washington, DC 20009
202/265-9500

Catholic University of America
Columbus School of Law
Washington, DC 20064
202/635-5144

Georgetown University
Law Center
600 New Jersey Ave., N.W.
Washington, DC 20001
202/624-8000

George Washington University
The National Law Center
720 20th Street, N.W.
Washington, DC 20052
202/676-6592

Howard University
School of Law
900 Van Ness Street, N.W.
Washington, DC 20008
202/686-6837

FLORIDA

Florida State University
College of Law
Tallahassee, FL 32306
904/644-3400

Nova Law Center
Goodwin Hall
3301 College Ave.
Ft. Lauderdale, FL 33315
305/522-2300

Stetson University
College of Law
1401 61st Street South
St. Petersburg, FL 33707
813/347-4560

University of Florida
College of Law
Spessard L. Holland Law Center
Gainesville, FL 32611
904/392-0421

University of Miami
School of Law
P. O. Box 2848087
Coral Gables, FL 33124
305/284-2392

GEORGIA

Emory University
School of Law
Atlanta, GA 30322
404/329-6815

Mercer University
Walter F. George School of Law
Macon, GA 31207
912/745-6811, ext. 343

University of Georgia
School of Law
Athens, GA 30602
404/542-7140

HAWAII

University of Hawaii
School of Law
1400 Lower Campus Road
Honolulu, HI 96822
808/948-7966

IDAHO

University of Idaho
College of Law
Moscow, ID 83843
208/885-6422

ILLINOIS

DePaul University
College of Law
25 East Jackson Blvd.
Chicago, IL 60604
312/321-7700

Illinois Institute of Technology
Chicago-Kent College of Law
77 South Wacker Drive
Chicago, IL 60606
312/567-5000

John Marshall Law School
315 South Plymouth Court
Chicago, IL 60604
312/427-2737

Loyola University
School of Law
One East Pearson St.
Chicago, IL 60611
312/670-2920

Northern Illinois University
College of Law
Glen Ellyn, IL 60137
312/858-7200

Northwestern University
School of Law
357 East Chicago Ave.
Chicago, IL 60611
312/649-8462

Southern Illinois University
School of Law
Carbondale, IL 62901
618/536-7711

University of Chicago
Law School
1111 East 60th St.
Chicago, IL 60637
312/753-2401

University of Illinois
College of Law
209 Law Building
Champaign, IL 61820
217/333-0930

INDIANA

Indiana University
School of Law
Bloomington, IN 47405
812/337-7995

Indiana University
School of Law – Indianapolis
735 West New York Street
Indianapolis, IN 46202
317/264-8523

University of Notre Dame
Law School
Notre Dame, IN 46556
219/283-6627

Valparaiso University
School of Law
Valparaiso, ID 46383
219/464-5436

IOWA

Drake University
Law School
Des Moines, IA 50311
515/271-2824

University of Iowa
College of Law
Iowa City, IA 52242
319/353-5742

KANSAS

University of Kansas
School of Law
New Green Hall
Lawrence, KS 66045
913/864-4550

Washburn University of Topeka
School of Law
1700 College Avenue
Topeka, KS 66621
913/295-6660

KENTUCKY

Northern Kentucky University
Salmon P. Chase College of Law
1401 Dixie Highway
Covington, KY 41011
606/292-5340

University of Kentucky
College of Law
Lexington, KY 40506
606/257-1678

University of Louisville
School of Law
Belknap Campus
2301 South Third Street
Louisville, KY 40208
502/588-6358

LOUISIANA

Louisiana State University
Law Center
Baton Rouge, LA 70803
504/388-8491

Loyola University
School of Law
6363 St. Charles Avenue
New Orleans, LA 70118
504/865-2261

Southern University
School of Law
Baton Rouge, LA 70813
504/771-3776

Tulane University
School of Law
New Orleans, LA 70118
504/866-2751

MAINE

University of Maine
School of Law
246 Deering Avenue
Portland, ME 04102
207/780-4340

MARYLAND

University of Baltimore
School of Law
Charles at Mt. Royal
Baltimore, MD 21201
301/727-6350, ext. 246

University of Maryland
School of Law
500 West Baltimore St.
Baltimore, MD 21201
301/528-7214

MASSACHUSETTS

Boston College
Law School
885 Centre Street
Newton Centre, MA 02159
617/969-0100

Boston University
School of Law
765 Commonwealth Ave.
Boston, MA 02215
617/353-3112

Harvard Law School
Cambridge, MA 02138
617/495-3100

New England School of Law
126 Newbury Street
Boston, MA 02116
617/267-9655

Northeastern University
School of Law
400 Huntington Avenue
Boston, MA 02115
617/437-3335

Suffolk University
Law School
41 Temple Street
Boston, MA 02114
617/723-4700

Western New England College
School of Law
54 Stuart St.
Springfield, MA 01119
617/451-0010

MICHIGAN

Detroit College of Law
130 East Elizabeth Street
Detroit, MI 48201
313/965-0150

Thomas M. Cooley Law School
217 South Capitol Ave.
Lansing, MI 48933
517/371-5140

University of Detroit
School of Law
651 East Jefferson Ave.
Detroit, MI 48226
313/961-5444

University of Michigan
Law School
South State Street
Ann Arbor, MI 48109
313/764-5278

Wayne State University
Law School
468 S. Ferry
Detroit, MI 48202
313/577-3930

MINNESOTA

Hamline University
School of Law
1536 Hewitt Avenue
St. Paul, MN 55104
612/641-2345

University of Minnesota
Law School
285 Law Building
Minneapolis, MN 55455
612/373-2717

William Mitchell College of Law
875 Summit Avenue
St. Paul, MN 55105
612/227-9171

MISSISSIPPI

University of Mississippi
School of Law
University, MS 38677
601/232-7361

MISSOURI

St. Louis University
School of Law
3700 Lindell Blvd.
St. Louis, MO 63108
314/658-2766

University of Missouri
School of Law
Tate Hall
Columbia, MO 65211
314/882-6487

University of Missouri
School of Law
5100 Rockhill Road
Kansas City, MO 64110
816/276-1644

Washington University
School of Law
St. Louis, MO 63130
314/889-6400

MONTANA

University of Montana
School of Law
Missoula, MT 59812
406/243-3411

NEBRASKA

Creighton University
School of Law
2133 California St.
Omaha, NB 68178
402/449-2872

University of Nebraska
College of Law
Lincoln, NB 68583
402/472-2161

NEW HAMPSHIRE

Franklin Pierce Law Center
2 White Street
Concord, NH 03301
603/228-1541

NEW JERSEY

Rutgers University
School of Law
Fifth and Penn Streets
Camden, NJ 08102
609/757-6398

Rutgers University
School of Law
15 Washington Street
Newark, NJ 07102
201/648-5561

Seton Hall University
School of Law
1111 Raymond Blvd.
Newark, NJ 07102
201/642-8500

NEW MEXICO

University of New Mexico
School of Law
1117 Stanford, N.E.
Albuquerque, NM 87131
505/277-2146

NEW YORK

Albany Law School
Union University
80 New Scotland Ave.
Albany, NY 12208
518/445-2311

Brooklyn Law School
250 Joralemon Street
Brooklyn, NY 11201
212/625-2200

Columbia University
School of Law
435 West 116th Street
New York, NY 10027
212/280-2671

Cornell Law School
Myron Taylor Hall
Ithaca, NY 14853
607/256-3626

Fordham University
School of Law
140 West 62nd Street
New York, NY 10023
212/841-5193

Hofstra University
School of Law
Hempstead, NY 11550
516/560-3636

New York Law School
57 Worth Street
New York, NY 10013
212/966-3500

New York University
School of Law
40 Washington Square, South
New York, NY 10012
212/598-2511

Pace University
School of Law
78 North Broadway
White Plains, NY 10603
914/682-7200

St. John's University
School of Law
Fromkes Hall
Jamaica, NY 11439
212/969-8000

State University of New York
   at Buffalo
School of Law
John Lord O'Brian Hall-
   Amherst Campus
Buffalo, NY 14260
716/636-2062

Syracuse University
College of Law
Ernest I. White Hall
Syracuse, NY 13210
315/423-2524

Yeshiva University
Benjamin N. Cardozo School of
   Law
Brookdale Center
55 Fifth Avenue
New York, NY 10003
212/790-0463

NORTH CAROLINA

Campbell University
School of Law
P.O. Box 158
Buies Creek, NC 27506
919/893-4111, ext. 342

Duke University
School of Law
Durham, NC 27706
919/684-2834

North Carolina Central Univ.
School of Law
1801 Fayetteville Street
Durham, NC 27707
919/683-6333

University of North Carolina
School of Law
Chapel Hill, NC 27514
919/933-5106

Wake Forest University
School of Law
Box 7206, Reynolds Station
Winston-Salem, NC 27109
919/761-5434

NORTH DAKOTA

University of North Dakota
School of Law
University Station
Grand Fork, ND 58202
701/777-2104

OHIO

Capital University
Law School
2199 East Main Street
Columbus, OH 43209
614/236-6395

Case Western Reserve Univ.
School of Law
11075 East Blvd.
Cleveland, OH 44106
216/368-3280

Cleveland State University
Cleveland-Marshall
    College of Law
Cleveland, OH 44115
216/687-2344

Ohio Northern University
Claude W. Pettit
    College of Law
Ada, OH 45810
419/634-9921

Ohio State University
College of Law
1659 North High St.
Columbus, OH 43210
614/422-2631

University of Akron
C. Blake McDowell Law Center
Akron, OH 44325
216/375-7331

University of Cincinnati
College of Law
13 Taft Hall
Cincinnati, OH 45221
513/475-6805

University of Dayton
School of Law
Dayton, OH 45469
513/229-3211

University of Toledo
College of Law
Toledo, OH 43606
419/537-2882

OKLAHOMA

Oklahoma City University
School of Law
Northwest 23rd and
    North Blackwelder
Oklahoma City, OK 73106
405/521-5337

University of Oklahoma
College of Law
300 Timberdell Road
Norman, OK 73019
405/329-8800

University of Tulsa
College of Law
3120 East Forth Place
Tulsa, OK 74104
918/592-6000, ext. 400

OREGON

Lewis and Clark College
Northwestern School of Law
10015 S.W. Terwilliger Blvd.
Portland, OR 97219
503/244-1181

University of Oregon
School of Law
1275 Kincaid Street
Eugene, OR 97403
503/686-3852

Willamette University
College of Law
Ferry and Winter St., S.E.
Salem, OR 97301
503/370-6380

PENNSYLVANIA

Dickinson School of Law
150 South College St.
Carlisle, PA 17013
717/243-4611

Duquesne University
School of Law
600 Forges Avenue
Pittsburg, PA 15219
412/434-6300

Temple University
School of Law
1719 North Broad St.
Philadelphia, PA 19122
215/787-7861

University of Pennsylvania
Law School
3400 Chestnut Street
Philadelphia, PA 19104
215/243-7483

University of Pittsburgh
School of Law
3900 Forbes Avenue
Pittsburgh, PA 15260
412/624-6200

Villanova University
School of Law
Villanova, PA 19085
215/527-2100

PUERTO RICO

Catholic University of
    Puerto Rico
School of Law
Ponce, PR 00731
809/844-4150, ext. 122

Inter-American University
    of Puerto Rico
School of Law
P. O. Box 8897
Fernandez Juncos Station
Santurce, PR 00910
809/727-1930

University of Puerto Rico
School of Law
Rio Piedras, PR 00931
809/764-6208

SOUTH CAROLINA

University of South Carolina
Law School
Main and Green Streets
Columbia, SC 29208
803/777-6617

SOUTH DAKOTA

University of South Dakota
School of Law
Vermillion, SD 57069
605/677-5361

TENNESSEE

Memphis State University
Cecil C. Humphreys School of Law
Memphis, TN 38152
901/454-2421

University of Tennessee
College of Law
1505 West Cumberland Ave.
Knoxville, TN 37916
615/974-4241

Vanderbilt University
School of Law
Nashville, TN 37240
615/322-2615

TEXAS

Baylor University
Law School
Waco, TX 76703
817/755-1911

St. Mary's University
School of Law
One Camino Santa Maria
San Antonio, TX 78284
512/436-3424

Southern Methodist University
School of Law
Dallas, TX 75275
214/692-2618

South Texas College of Law
1303 San Jacinto Street
Houston, TX 77002
713/659-8040

Texas Southern University
Thurgood Marshall
School of Law
3201 Wheeler Ave.
Houston, TX 77004
713/527-7112

Texas Tech University
School of Law
P. O. Box 4030
Lubbock, TX 79409
806/742-3791

University of Houston
Bates College of Law
Houston, TX 77004
713/749-1422

University of Texas
School of Law
2500 Red River
Austin, TX 78705
512/471-5151

UTAH

Brigham Young University
J. Reuben Clark Law School
Provo, UT 84602
801/374-1211, ext. 4274

University of Utah
College of Law
Salt Lake City, UT 84112
801/581-6833

VERMONT

Vermont Law School
South Royalton, VT 05068
802/763-8303

VIRGINIA

College of William and Mary
Marshal-Wythe School of Law
Williamsburg, VA 23185
804/253-4509

Judge Advocate General's School
(Post-J.D. programs only)
U.S. Army
Charlottesville, VA 22901
804/977-4930

University of Richmond
School of Law
Richmond, VA 23173
804/285-6336

University of Virginia
School of Law
Charlottesville, VA 22901
804/924-7343

Washington and Lee University
School of Law
Lewis Hall
Lexington, VA 24450
703/463-9111

WASHINGTON

Gonzaga University
School of Law
East 702 Sharp
P. O. Box 3528
Spokane, WA 99202
509/326-5310

University of Puget Sound
School of Law
8811 South Tacoma Way
Tacoma, WA 98499
206/756-3322

University of Washington
School of Law
Condon Hall, JB-20
1100 N.E. Campus Pkwy.
Seattle, WA 98105
206/543-4550

WEST VIRGINIA

West Virginia University
College of Law
Law Center
Morgantown, WV 26506
304/293-5306

WISCONSIN

Marquette University
Law School
1103 West Wisconsin Ave.
Milwaukee, WI 53233
414/224-7090

University of Wisconsin
Law School
Madison, WI 53706
608/262-2240

WYOMING

University of Wyoming
College of Law
P. O. Box 3035
University Station
Laramie, WY 82071
307/766-6416

APPENDIX B

Attorney/Population Ratios

STATE	POPULATION (1980 est.)	ATTORNEYS	PERSONS PER LAWYER
Alabama	3,691,000	4,591	803.96
Alaska	413,000	1,269	325.45
Arizona	2,305,000	4,585	502.73
Arkansas	2,152,000	3,102	693.75
California	21,887,000	59,896	365.42
Colorado	2,625,000	6,853	383.04
Connecticut	3,107,000	7,520	
Delaware	582,000	899	647.39
District of Columbia	685,000	28,200	224.29
Florida	8,466,000	18,015	469.94
Georgia	5,041,000	9,841	512.24
Hawaii	891,000	1,974	451.37
Idaho	856,000	1,355	631.73
Illinois	11,228,000	26,642	421.44
Indiana	5,350,000	7,352	729.69
Iowa	2,888,000	5,152	560.56
Kansas	2,320,000	4,136	560.93
Kentucky	3,468,000	5,623	616.75
Louisiana	3,930,000	7,974	492.85
Maine	1,084,000	1,774	611.05

STATE	POPULATION (1980 est.)	ATTORNEYS	PERSONS PER LAWYER
Massachusetts	5,777,000	16,576	348.52
Michigan	9,148,000	15,901	575.31
Minnesota	3,980,000	8,136	489.18
Mississippi	2,386,000	3,478	686.03
Missouri	4,822,000	9,291	519.00
Montana	766,000	1,429	536.04
Nebraska	1,555,000	3,024	514.22
Nevada	637,000	1,245	511.65
New Hampshire	850,000	1,532	554.83
New Jersey	7,338,000	17,363	422.62
New Mexico	1,196,000	2,335	512.21
New York	17,932,000	61,100	293.49
North Carolina	5,515,000	7,862	701.48
North Dakota	650,000	1,005	646.77
Ohio	10,696,000	22,123	483.48
Oklahoma	2,817,000	6,332	444.88
Oregon	2,385,000	5,009	476.14
Pennsylvania	11,796,000	20,735	568.89
Rhode Island	937,000	2,124	441.15
South Carolina	2,878,000	3,904	737.19
South Dakota	688,000	1,322	520.42
Tennessee	4,292,000	6,168	695.85
Texas	12,806,000	27,072	473.03
Utah	1,270,000	2,358	538.59
Vermont	482,000	893	539.75
Virginia	5,095,000	8,947	569.46
Washington	3,681,000	9,588	383.92
West Virginia	1,853,000	2,224	833.18
Wisconsin	4,644,000	7,520	617.55
Wyoming	406,000	753	539.18

APPENDIX C

Proposed Model Rules of Professional Conduct: Preamble American Bar Association

A lawyer is an officer of the legal system, a representative of clients, and a public citizen having special responsibility for the quality of justice.

A lawyer's conduct should conform to the requirements of the law, both in professional service to clients and in the lawyer's business and personal affairs. A lawyer should use the law's procedures only for legitimate purposes and not to harass or intimidate others. A lawyer should demonstrate respect for the legal system and for those who serve it, including judges, other lawyers, and public officials in general. While it is a lawyer's duty, when necessary, to challenge the rectitude of official action, it is also a lawyer's duty to uphold legal process.

As a representative of clients, a lawyer performs various functions. As adviser, a lawyer should provide a client with an informed understanding of the client's legal rights and their practical implications. A lawyer's advice should include consideration of the client's legal obligations and the interests of other persons who may be affected in the circumstances. A lawyer should seek to dissuade clients from conduct wrongful to others and should not lend assistance to such purposes.

As advocate, a lawyer should diligently assert the client's position while being honest with the tribunal and showing proper respect for the interests of opposing parties and other concerned persons.

133

As negotiator, a lawyer should seek a result advantageous to the client but consistent with requirements of fair dealing with others. A lawyer should safeguard the client's interest and may ordinarily assume that opposing parties in a transaction are adequately represented or adequately represent themselves. However, when an opposing party is manifestly incapable of protecting his or her own interests, on account of ignorance, adversity of circumstance, or other reason, a lawyer should moderate a client's demands so as to avoid a legally unconscionable result.

A lawyer may serve as intermediary between clients by seeking to reconcile their divergent interests. As intermediary, a lawyer is an adviser and, to a limited extent, spokesman for each client, promoting accommodation between them.

A lawyer acts as evaluator by examining a client's legal affairs and reporting about them to the client or to others. If the evaluation is to be relied on by others, the lawyer assumes a professional duty not only to the client but also to third persons.

In all professional relationships a lawyer should act competently, promptly, and diligently. A lawyer should keep confidential all information relating to clients except so far as disclosure is appropriate in the service of a client or is required or permitted by law or these Rules of Professional Conduct.

As a public citizen, a lawyer should seek improvement of the law, the administration of justice, and the quality of service rendered by the legal profession. As a member of a learned profession, a lawyer should cultivate knowledge of the law beyond its use for clients, employ that knowledge in reform of the law, and work to strengthen legal education. A lawyer should be mindful of deficiencies in the administration of justice and of the fact that the poor, and sometimes persons who are not poor, cannot afford adequate legal assistance, and should therefore devote professional time and civic influence in their behalf. A lawyer should aid the legal profession in seeking these objectives and should help the bar regulate itself in the public interest.

Many of a lawyer's professional responsibilities are legal duties and are prescribed in the Rules of Professional Conduct. However, a lawyer also has professional obligations regulated by personal conscience and the approbation of professional peers. These include practicing at a lawyer's highest level of skill, devoting effort to improving the law and the legal profession, and striving to exemplify the legal profession's ideals of public service.

A lawyer's responsibilities as an officer of the court, a representative of clients, and a public citizen are usually harmonious. Thus, when an opposing party is well represented, a lawyer can be a vigorous advocate on behalf of a client and at the same time assume that justice is being done. So also, a lawyer can be sure that preserving client confidences ordinarily serves the public interest because people are more likely to seek legal advice, and thereby heed their legal obligations, when they know they can do so in private.

In the nature of law practice, however, conflicting responsibilities are encountered. Virtually all difficult ethical problems arise from conflict in a lawyer's responsibilities, including responsibilities to clients, to the legal system, to the general public, and to the lawyer's own interest in remaining an upright person while earning a satisfactory living. The Rules of Professional Conduct prescribe terms for resolving these conflicts. Nevertheless, many of the difficult choices call for exercise of sensitive professional and moral judgment in which lawyers must be guided by the basic principles underlying the Rules of Professional Conduct.

APPENDIX D

Approval of Law Schools
American Bar Association
Standards and Rules of Procedures
(Selected Standards)

211:   The law school shall maintain equality of opportunity in legal education without discrimination or segregation on the ground of race, color, religion, national origin, or sex.

(c)   Equality of opportunity in legal education includes equal opportunity to obtain employment. Each school should communicate to every employer to whom it furnishes assistance and facilities for interviewing and other placement functions the school's firm expectation that the employer will observe the principle of equal opportunity and will avoid objectionable practices such as

(i)   refusing to hire or promote members of the groups protected by this policy because of the prejudices of clients or or professional or official associates;

(ii) applying standards in the hiring and promoting of such individuals that are higher than those applied otherwise;

(iii) maintaining a starting or promotional salary scale as to such individuals that is lower than is applied otherwise; and

(iv) disregarding personal capabilities by assigning, in a predetermined or mechanical manner, such individuals to certain kinds of work or departments.

213:   The law school should provide adequate staff, space, and resources in view of the size and program of the school to maintain an active placement service to assist its graduates to make sound career choices.

301: (a) The law school shall maintain an educational program that is designed to qualify its graduates for admission to the bar.

302: (a) The law school shall offer:

(i) instruction in those subjects generally regarded as the core of the law school curriculum,

(ii) training in professional skills, such as counselling, the drafting of legal documents and materials, and trial and appellate advocacy,

(iii) and shall provide and require for all student candidates for a professional degree, instruction in the duties and responsibilities of the legal profession. Such required instruction need not be limited to any pedagogical method as long as the history, goals, structure and responsibilities of the legal profession and its members, including the ABA Code of Professional Responsibility, are all covered. Each law school is encouraged to involve members of the bench and bar in such instruction.

(b) The law school may not offer to its students for academic credit or as a condition to graduation, instruction that is designed as a bar examination review course.

303: (a) The educational program of the law school should provide for:

(i) study in seminars or by directed research,

(ii) small classes for at least some portion of the total instructional program.

APPENDIX E

Sample Law School Exam Question

The following question actually appeared on a law school Criminal Law examination for a first year course:

Defendant Accomplice was in the illegal drug business with Defendant Principal. While in State A, Principal shot over the border (a river) into State B and killed Agent Officer, who was an FBI agent. State A gave transactional immunity to Accomplice for the murder charge for his agreement to testify against Principal. Accomplice testified before the grand jury in State A that he had observed Principal shoot and kill Officer.

State B by information and the Federal Government by indictment charged Accomplice jointly with Principal for the murder of Officer. State B made their charges on the basis of the death of Officer within its borders, and the federal charge was based on the fact the victim was a federal agent.

State B officers went over to State A and arrested Accomplice for the murder of Officer. He was searched, but nothing of significance was found on him at that time. However, after he was booked at the police station in State B, his clothing was searched more thoroughly and in his wallet a piece of paper—which was an unfinished letter to his mother—was found. In the letter he stated he had helped kill Officer.

State B Police gave Accomplice Miranda warnings—which he stated he understood—and said he was willing to talk with the police. They said they knew he had testified before the grand jury in State A, and he then confessed. He was then brought before the State B court for a preliminary examination and while in court he was observed by Officer's wife—who had seen her husband shot—and she recognized Accomplice as one who drove an automobile away with Principal in it, after Principal had shot her husband. Principal also confessed to the police implicating Accomplice.

(1) You are appointed counsel for Accomplice in State B court before arraignment. What motions will you make in relation to the murder charges? What would be the expected rulings? Give your reasons. Consider only United States Constitutional and jurisdictional issues on the assumption that no State constitutional, statutory or court rules have been violated. Please number the motions. You are expected to know whether motions are made pretrial, during trial or post-trial, but you are expected to make all motions that are raised by (but also limited by) the facts given above.

(2) Assume that Accomplice is acquitted in State B by your brilliant defense, but Principal was convicted. The Federal Justice Department decides to prosecute because of the acquittal. You continue your defense of Accomplice in federal court. Among other motions you request a copy of the State B trial transcript for defense purposes, but you discover that the tape recordings of the trial have been erased and thus a transcript is unavailable. What motions involving constitutional issues would you make in federal court and what rulings would you expect from the federal district court. Any motions which would be the same in federal court as in state court (and for which you would not expect any different rulings or give different reasoning), please just refer back to the motion number you made in state court.

GLOSSARY

The following terms used in this book are defined in this glossary for easy reference by the reader. They not only define more clearly expressions used in the text, but also stand to provide an easy guide to "legalese" with which many readers may not be familiar.

ABA —The American Bar Association. A national voluntary association of lawyers with a membership in excess of 250,000 members. The ABA is reputed to be the largest voluntary professional organization in the world.

ACCREDITED LAW SCHOOL —Although the term is sometimes used loosely, an accredited law school has been approved by the American Bar Association through an intensive inspection process; in most jurisdictions only graduates of ABA-approved schools may take the Bar Examination. Since the ABA is certified by the U. S. Department of Education to grant such approval, only ABA-approved schools can be considered accredited.

ADVERTISING —When used by lawyers, the term advertising generally refers to the right of lawyers to advertise to the public the availability to provide legal services as enunciated in the case of *Bates and O'Steen v. Arizona.*

ALTERNATIVE PRACTICE —One of a number of areas of practice which are considered non-traditional. This definition is quite subjective, and the jobs included will vary depending on the individual. Usually alternative practice is a euphemism for legal aid, legal services and public interest practice (and that is how it is used in this book), although some people also include any law-related employment not in a law firm, corporate counsels' office, or government agency.

ASSOCIATE –A junior lawyer in a law firm who is generally salaried, although some associates in some firms may participate in the earnings of the firm.

BACCALAUREATE DEGREE –The degree awarded at the completion of a four to five year college curriculum; a bachelor's degree (e.g., B.A., B.S., B.B.A., B.F.A., A.B.); the lowest educational level of degree held by students entering law school.

BAKKE –(pronounced Bah' key) *Bakke v. The Board of Regents of the University of California at Davis* is a case decided by the United States Supreme Court on the question of admission standards to professional schools. Bakke, a white applicant to the California-Davis Medical School, was denied admission to the school even though minority students whose index scores were not comparable to his own were admitted. He argued that the school had engaged in reverse discrimination by admitting less qualified minorities to his detriment. The Court ruled that Bakke should be admitted because the school's quota system for admitting minority students was unconstitutional. However, the Court also held that affirmative action plans by professional schools which took into account factors other than test scores and college grades in order to identify qualified candidates from groups underrepresented in the schools' population were constitutional. Although the entire opinion is very complex and confusing even to legal scholars, the practical result has been that law schools now look at many subjective factors such as motivation, work experience, extra-curricular activities, school attended, major and minority group status, to name a few.

BAR EXAM –The test given to law school graduates before they are licensed to practice law; each state has its own bar exam, so law practice is limited to those jurisdictions in which an individual has passed the bar.

BILLABLE HOURS –The number of hours a lawyer works and bills to a client.

BY THE NUMBERS —In law school admissions, a practice by which applicants are considered solely on the basis of grade point average (GPA) and LSAT score, usually combined into an index. This method of selection may produce law school classes which have higher median scores with individuals in them who are less well-rounded, and arguably less qualified to practice law.

CAREER —The sum of an individual's working experience. Generally a career is thought of in terms of jobs, but should properly not be so limited.

CAREER DEVELOPMENT —The idea that a career has a direction or pattern that ideally should reflect the personal and professional growth of the individual as time passes.

CAREER OPTIONS —The choices available to persons in a professional field, generally those positions where one's education and experience prepare him/her for the work that will be involved on the job.

CAREER PLANNING —The concept of making rational career decisions on the basis of careful self-evaluation and analysis of the job market.

CLE —Continuing Legal Education. Programs offered to practicing lawyers to update or refine their skills in and knowledge of the law.

CLERKSHIP —1. A position held by a law graduate working for a judge for one to two years after graduation before taking a permanent job. 2. A summer or part-time job with a legal employer during law school doing research and other legal work for attorneys in the organization.

CLIENT —An individual, corporation, government or other business organization utilizing a lawyer's services.

CLINICAL LEGAL EDUCATION —Courses in law school in which students handle actual legal problems under the supervision of professors or practicing lawyers instead of merely answering hypothetical problems; all law schools have some clinical programs but they vary widely in their size, scope, and orientation.

CODE OF PROFESSIONAL RESPONSIBILITY —A document promulgated by the American Bar Association nationally, and followed closely in the various states, which defines the lawyer's ethical responsibilities. Violation of these rules may lead to discipline by the authority which licenses attorneys, usually the Supreme Court of the State.

CONTRACTS —A branch of the law involving agreements among people and organizations, including when agreements are enforceable in law and what liability results from their breach; one of the primary first year law school courses is Contracts.

CORPORATE COUNSEL —A lawyer on the legal staff of a corporation.

CULTURAL BIAS —In the area of standardized tests, this is where members of cultural or minority groups score lower on a test because of their background as members of that group; many minority students score lower on the LSAT than Anglos, giving rise to the charge that the LSAT is culturally biased.

ENTREPRENEUR —An individual who establishes his/her own business.

GENERAL COUNSEL —The chief lawyer in a business or government organization.

GPA —The college grade point average is used along with the Law School Admission Test (See LSAT) in selecting students to be admitted to law school.

GROUP LEGAL SERVICES —Legal services provided to members of a group (e.g. an employee's union) by staff attorneys as a part of the benefits available to members of the group.

HANGING OUT A SHINGLE —Opening an individual private practice.

HYPO —Short for hypothetical situation, a case made up by the law professor to illustrate a point, deriving from hypothesis. Example—"Assume that I promise to give you $50 to walk across the Brooklyn Bridge and you agree. Now, when you get three-fourths of the way across the bridge, I change my mind and revoke the offer. Can you sue me for the entire amount? For part of it? For your lost time?"

IN-HOUSE COUNSEL —In a corporation or agency, a lawyer or legal department that is on the staff of the corporation or agency, as opposed to outside counsel. A lawyer who works for a private law firm whose client is a corporation.

INTERNSHIP —A legal job during law school for which academic credit is given, and which usually involves supervision by a professor in addition to the practitioner employing the student.

JAGC —Judge Advocate General Corps. The legal arm of the military services.

JD —The basic law degree required to be completed in order to qualify to sit for the bar exam, usually requiring 3-4 years of study after graduation from college.

JOINT DEGREE —A program in which a law school offers a curriculum leading to degrees in law and another field, most commonly a graduate level degree in business administration.

JUDICIAL ADMINISTRATION —The mangement of the court system; a career involving such management.

LAW CLINICS —Law offices set up to provide inexpensive legal services to people of moderate means by routinizing and standardizing services in such a way as to lower costs while maintaining quality.

LAW FIRM —A group of two or more lawyers in private practice of law; the members of the firm are generally called partners or shareholders and the salaried lawyers, associates.

LAW-RELATED JOB —A job which is frequently filled by a lawyer and for which a legal education is valuable training, but which does not require that the law graduate holding the job be licensed to practice law by passing a bar exam.

LAW REVIEW —A journal published by a law school which contains academic analysis of legal questions and recent cases; the law reviews are student-edited by students selected on the basis of grades and/or writing competition.

LEGAL AID —A term frequently used to describe a program offering legal services to indigent or poverty level clients (See legal services).

LEGAL SERVICES —1. A general term used to describe the work that lawyers provide for clients (e.g. a lawyer is in the business of offering legal services to clients). 2. A more specific term used to describe a program offering legal services for indigent or poverty level individuals (e.g. the National Legal Services Corporation). Although used interchangeably with the term legal aid, legal services is becoming increasingly popular despite the confusing definition.

LITIGATION —An area of law practice involving the trial of law suits, the work also refers to any adversary trial in the courts where parties are represented by attorneys in an adversary relationship.

L.L.M. —Master of Laws—a postgraduate law degree obtained through 1-2 years of law school after the Juris Doctor (See JD).

LOCAL LAW SCHOOL —Euphemism describing a law school's reputation as neither a national nor regional school; a school where graduates are recruited usually by legal employers from the city where the school is located.

LSAT —The Law School Admission Test is an exam given to persons interested in attending law school. The LSAT is designed to test aptitude for doing legal work. While its effectiveness has been disputed, it is used as a major criterion for determining which applicants will be admitted to law school each year.

MEDIAN —The middle value in a set of ordered values; thus a median salary or LSAT score means that half the salaries or scores fall above and half below the median.

MOOT COURT —A law school activity involving a competition in which students write briefs and orally argue hypothetical cases before moot court judges.

NATIONAL LAW SCHOOLS —Euphemism describing a law school's reputation as being recognized as one of the best law schools in the nation; a school whose graduates are recruited by legal employers from throughout the country.

NIGHT SCHOOL —Some law schools have a part-time program in the evening for students who must work their way through school; such a program normally takes four years to complete instead of three necessary for full-time students.

NO-FAULT —A system of compensation for victims of accidents which does not rely upon negligence as a basis of liability, and in so doing eliminates expensive personal injury litigation.

NON-LEGAL JOB —A job in which a law graduate does not

practice law or specifically use his/her law training. Law school may provide a general background and training for the position.

PARTNER —One of the members of a law firm; the partners are the owners of the business; the shareholders in a professional corporation are sometimes called partners.

PERSONAL INJURY —An area of law practice involving litigation produced as a result of some injury to an individual. PI, as it is called, usually involves negligence on the part of one of the parties, resulting in the injury to the other, and in most cases today insurance is involved.

POPULATION/ATTORNEY RATIO —The population of a given area divided by the number of attorneys in that area; a figure that is frequently used to assess the relative abundance of lawyers.

PRE-LAW MAJOR —A student in college who is preparing to attend law school. There are very few schools which offer a course of study in "pre-law" which would lead to a degree as in English or Business, so the term properly describes only the students themselves who may be in any field of study.

PREPAID LEGAL SERVICES —Legal services provided to persons or families who participate in a plan under which they make monthly contributions and receive benefits designated under the plan. Prepaid legal insurance works very much like Blue Cross/Blue Shield in the health field.

PRIVATE PRACTICE —An individual or organization engaged in the business of delivering legal services for compensation.

PRO BONO PUBLICO —(Latin—for the public good). A term sometimes used interchangeably with public interest, but also used to refer to the lawyer's responsibility to perform work in the public interest. The organized bar is divided as to the extent and limits of this responsibility.

PROPERTY —A branch of the law dealing with ownership of land, objects (chattels), ideas, or anything including what can be owned, and what rights are associated with ownership; one of the primary first year law school courses is Property.

PUBLIC DEFENDER —The attorney who works in the criminal service branch of legal service for the indigent. Since the U.S. Supreme Court case of *Gideon v. Wainwright* every person who is accused of a crime is guaranteed the right to legal representation. Many jurisdictions fund public defender offices for accused persons who cannot afford to retain private counsel.

PUBLIC INTEREST PRACTICE —A law practice in which the lawyer's clients are not normal paying individuals or corporations, but the public at large; in some cases certain special interest groups promote their causes as public interest (See also Pro Bono Publico).

REGIONAL LAW SCHOOL —Euphemism describing a law school's reputation as being recognized as one of the best law schools in a state or region; a school whose graduates are recruited predominantly by legal employers from the region where the school is located.

SKILLS —In the career choice process skills are the things that you can do: think of them as action verbs, and as transferable; they represent the things you will be required to do working in a particular profession such as law.

SOCRATIC METHOD —A teaching method used in American law schools since the 19th century in which the professor, using either written decisions of appellate courts or hypothetical situations, teaches by means of intense questioning of students concerning the cases. Named for the Greek philosopher Socrates, who taught by using a question-answer format, and introduced into legal education at Harvard Law

School, the Socratic method in recent years has been supplemented in most law schools by traditional lectures, practical or clinical programs, seminars, and problem-solving research courses.

SOLE PRACTITIONER —(also solo practitioner). An individual lawyer in private practice.

SPECIALIZATION —The development of a practice of law limited to a narrow field of expertise, an increasing phenomenon in the legal profession today.

SUBSTANTIVE LAW —An area of law practice defined by its subject matter (e.g., energy law, admiralty law).

TAX LAW —An area of law practice which involves the complex and pervasive federal and state taxation laws.

TORT —(French N.—Wrong) An area of law dealing with injuries. While most tort law deals with negligent acts which result in injuries, there are also intentional torts and torts in which negligence need not be shown before liability can be established. One of the primary first year law school courses is in Torts.

UNDEREMPLOYED —A term referring to a person who believes that his or her job is not utilizing legal skills adequately. While this term clearly covers those who have accepted non-legal jobs although they wanted legal ones, it can also be used to refer to anyone who is not satisfied with his or her present job.

UNEMPLOYED —In the legal profession, a person who is actively seeking a legal or law-related job but cannot find one, and is not employed.

WORK VALUES —Those basic needs and attitudes which determine satisfaction in a professional career choice or job, e.g., independence, power, wealth, altruism.

BIBLIOGRAPHY

American Bar Association, Section of Legal Education and Admissions to the Bar, *Review of Legal Education*, Chicago: American Bar Association (Annual, 1979).

American Bar Association Section on International Law, *Career Opportunities in International Law*, Chicago: American Bar Association (1977).

American Bar Association Standing Committee on Professional Utilization and Career Development, *Non-Legal Careers: New Opportunities for Lawyers*, Chicago: American Bar Association (1979).

Ashell, Bernard, *What Lawyers Really Do*, New York: P. H. Wydon Co. (1970).

Ashman, Allan, *The New Private Practice*, Chicago: National Legal Aid and Defender Association (1972).

Association of American Law Schools and the Law School Admission Council, *The Pre-Law Handbook*, Indianapolis, Bobbs Merrill (Annual, 1980).

Balancing the Scales of Justice: Financing Public Interest Law in America, Washington, D.C.: Council for Public Interest Law (1976).

Bolles, Richard N., *What Color Is Your Parachute?* Berkeley: Ten Speed Press (Annual, 1979).

Brakel, Samuel J., *Judiacare: Public Funds, Private Lawyers, and Poor People*, Chicago: American Bar Foundation (1974).

Carlin, Jerome E., *Lawyers on Their Own*, New Brunswick: Rutgers University Press (1962).

Christianson, Barlow F., *Lawyers for People of Moderate Means: Some Problems of Availability of Legal Services*, Chicago: American Bar Foundation (1970).

Clark, Christine P., *Minority Opportunities in Law for Blacks, Puerto Ricans, and Chicanos*, New York: Law Journal Press (1974).

Class of 1979 Employment Report, Sacramento: National Association for Law Placement (Annual, 1979).